DATE LOANED

MAR 1 7 1993	DEC 0 2 2004	
APR 1 6 1993		
APR 1 5		
JUL 1 0 1993		
JUL 1 0		
AUG 21 '93		
JUN 27 '95		
JUN 2 1		
OCT 1 5 1997		
SEP 2 6 REC'D 1997		
DEC 1 1 1997		
NOV 2 1 REC'D		
FEB 2 6 1998		
OCT 3 0 2000		
NOV 2 0 2000		
NOV 0 7 2000		

The Films Of The Forties

The Films

ALSO BY TONY THOMAS
The Films of Kirk Douglas
The Films of Marlon Brando
Song and Dance Man: The Films of Gene Kelly
The Films of Errol Flynn (*co-author*)
Harry Warren and the Hollywood Musical

Of The Forties

Tony Thomas

A CITADEL PRESS BOOK   PUBLISHED BY CAROL PUBLISHING GROUP

First Carol Publishing Group Edition 1990

Copyright © 1975 by Tony Thomas

A Citadel Press Book
Published by Carol Publishing Group

Editorial Offices
600 Madison Avenue
New York, NY 10022

Sales & Distribution Offices
120 Enterprise Avenue
Secaucus, NJ 07094

In Canada: Musson Book Company
A division of General Publishing Co. Limited
Don Mills, Ontario

Manufactured in the United States of America
ISBN 0-8065-0741-4

10 9 8 7 6

Acknowledgments

Much of the research for this book was done either at the library of The Academy of Motion Picture Arts and Sciences in Los Angeles, where I am once again indebted to Mildred Simpson and her staff, and at the Ontario Film Institute in Toronto, with the kind cooperation of Gerald Pratley and his staff. In the all-important task of finding the many photographs needed for this book, I am grateful to John Lebold, Gunnard Nelson, Eddie Brandt, Diane Goodrich, Bob Colman, and the Larry Edmonds Bookstore (Hollywood). Without these facilities and this help the project could not have been realized.

Contents

The Films Of The Forties

Explaining The Choice

Perhaps I should begin with a few words about what this book is and what it isn't. This is a personal assessment of one hundred major feature films produced in Hollywood in the 1940s. I have hoped to give a comprehensive account of just one level of creativity in those years—Hollywood's upper level. However, there were many other areas of great productivity—B pictures, cartoons, shorts, newsreels, and the trailers. I hope this book may inspire someone to cover those other celluloid regions, populated by Blondie, the Bowery Boys, Dr. Kildare, Maisie, Charlie Chan, Sherlock Holmes, Tarzan, James Fitzpatrick, Joe McDoaks, the Wolf Man, and Westbrook Van Vorhees' stentorian narration of *The March of Time.* They were all as much a part of movie programming in the forties as the main features.

The greatest difficulty in life, according to philosophers, is making choices, and I need no philosopher to tell me how painful it has been to select one hundred items from Hollywood's richest and most fruitful period. The seven major studios—Metro-Goldwyn-Mayer, Twentieth Century-Fox, Warner

Bros., Paramount, Universal, Columbia, and RKO-Radio—turned out approximately four hundred features a year during the forties. I found it difficult to list more than 10 percent of these as films of enduring merit and interest. Whittling down my initial list of four hundred to those contained between these covers caused much anguish, and I am not sure I shall ever be fully satisfied with my own selection.

This is not an eccentric listing. Many of these films would appear in most selections of the best Hollywood features of the forties. But there are some glaring omissions, and they are intentional. Such magnificent pictures as *Citizen Kane, Casablanca, The Best Years of Our Lives, The Great Dictator, Yankee Doodle Dandy,* and *The Treasure of the Sierra Madre* have been so fully discussed elsewhere that any comment from me would be superfluous. Please assume that they are at the unseen head of my list.

In arriving at a balanced selection I limited myself to just a representative few films directed by Alfred Hitchcock and John Ford, and in the case of certain major stars I rationed myself to one picture apiece. The careers of such great favorites as Bette Davis, James Cagney, Spencer Tracy, Joan Crawford, Clark Gable, Gary Cooper, and Cary Grant have all been the subjects of books, notably Citadel Press's *The Films of . . .* series, and I strove here to cover many personalities who have not been included in these compendiums. In making my structure fit as many aspects of movie popularity as possible, I regret that I could not include the contributions of Abbott and Costello, Gene Autry, Roy Rogers, Sonja Henie, Wallace Beery, and Esther Williams, all of whom attained top-ten status at the box office.

Nostalgia is tricky. Distance does indeed lend enchantment to the view, and I have many times been disappointed to find that a fondly remembered picture had far less appeal than I had remembered. I was a young and avid moviegoer in the forties, but in choosing the films for this book I was not relying on memory. I have become more than a little reacquainted with them, and none needs defending. What strikes me most forcibly is their high quality of craftsmanship. The studios were affluent and powerful during the forties, and their success had enabled them to put together companies of great talents—actors, directors, writers, photographers, composers, set designers, and sound technicians—to turn out entertainment for a vast market. Those times, to state the very obvious, are no more. The studio systems, with all their built-in securities, are long gone, and filmmaking, for both better and worse, is now the most open of markets.

The forties were, with room for academic argument, the years of Hollywood's greatest productivity and its last great decade. The decade began with feelings of uncertainly—Hollywood was ever subject to the tremors of doubts and fears—as the Second World War caused the movie markets to diminish, and it ended with even greater doubts and fears. By the end of 1949 it was obvious that television would become a major entertainment industry and draw millions away from their moviegoing habits. Also, to Hollywood's grief the U.S. government finally exercised its antitrust laws and forced the studios to divest themselves of their chains of theaters, which had given them block-booking distribution and almost automatic profits. Adding to the miseries of the moguls were the severe demands of the trade unions, which would drastically increase the costs of production, and the political witchhunts that brought feelings of disgust and dissent. The forties spelled the end of the old Hollywood, but between the extremes of 1940 and 1949 came a canyon of plenty.

I can only hope that my selection from this boom period will please others as much as it pleases me.

TONY THOMAS

3

Burgess Meredith and Betty Field.

Of Mice and Men.

1940

A United Artists Release; produced and directed by Lewis Milestone; screenplay by Eugene Solow, based on the book by John Steinbeck; photographed by Norbert Brodine; musical score by Aaron Copland; running time, 107 minutes.

Cast: Burgess Meredith (*George*), Betty Field (*Mae*), Lon Chaney, Jr. (*Lennie*), Charles Bickford (*Slim*), Roman Bohnen (*Candy*), Bob Steele (*Curley*), Noah Beery, Jr. (*Whit*), Oscar O'Shea (*Jackson*). Granville Bates (*Carlson*), Leigh Whipper (*Crooks*), Leona Roberts (*Aunt Clara*), Helen Lynd (*Susie*), Barbara Pepper (*Second Girl*), Henriette Kaye (*Third Girl*), Eddie Dunn (*Bus Driver*), Howard Mitchell (*Sheriff*).

The impression of American life Hollywood gave the world in its thousands of dramas, comedies, musicals, and Westerns was largely false. To people in other countries the United States seemed populated by gangsters, cowboys, lighthearted adventurers, and an unusually high percentage of wealthy citizens. The movie moguls could argue that their enormous profits came from entertaining customers, not from educating them.

In 1940, however, Hollywood producers began to take a different attitude toward classic American literature, possibly because the loss of European markets caused them to recognize the need for greater esteem for their products within the United States. This change in policy, abetted by many critics and public bodies, resulted in at least three excellent examples of film Americana in 1940: Thornton Wilder's *Our Town* and two treatments of John Steinbeck novels, the justly celebrated *The Grapes of Wrath*, directed by John Ford, and *Of Mice and Men*, directed with realism and taste by Lewis Milestone.

Steinbeck's story concerns the adventures of a pair of drifters who work as seasonal farm hands in California and often end up in trouble because of brawling. George is an easygoing but crafty fellow, and Lennie is a dim brute of a man, childishly dependent on George. Most of the action takes place on a San Joaquin Valley barley ranch. The pugnacious owner is aware that his sexy wife has a hankering for healthy ranch hands and they for her, and tragedy arises from her flirting with Lennie. In a confusion of affection and anger he kills her. (The film has established that the incredibly strong simpleton has several times unintentionally crushed the life out of animals while affectionately caressing them.) Rather than turn Lennie in to the law, George kills him, in much the way that a man would end the life of a sick animal.

Of Mice and Men is excellent on all counts. Its photography affords fine insights into California farming and its producers were inspired in hiring Aaron Copland to write a sensitive, evocative musical score. The casting is without fault, with Burgess Meredith as the wily George, Betty Field as the slatternly wife, and, in the performance of his career, Lon Chaney, Jr., as Lennie. At no other point in his forty years in the movies did Chaney equal this poignant performance.

Charles Bickford, Howard Mitchell and Burgess Meredith.

Lon Chaney, Jr., Charles Bickford and Bob Steele.

George Murphy, Eleanor Powell and Fred Astaire.

Broadway Melody of 1940

1940

An MGM Production; produced by Jack Cummings; directed by Norman Taurog; screenplay by Leon Gordon and George Oppenheimer, based on a story by Jack MacGowan and Dore Schary; photographed by Oliver T. Marsh and Joseph Ruttenberg; songs by Cole Porter; musical direction by Alfred Newman; running time, 102 minutes.

Cast: Fred Astaire (*Johnny Brett*), Eleanor Powell (*Clara Brett*), George Murphy (*King Shaw*), Frank Morgan (*Bon Casey*), Ian Hunter (*Bert C. Mathews*), Florence Rice (*Amy Blake*), Lynne Carver (*Emmy Lou Lee*), Ann Morriss (*Pearl*), Trixie Firschke (*Juggler*), Douglas McPhail (*Masked Singer*).

Fred Astaire and George Murphy.

In 1939 Fred Astaire found himself in the same dilemma he had faced eight years previously—the lack of a dancing partner. In 1931 his sister Adele had married and retired, after the two had been a team for more than twenty years. Now, after Astaire and Ginger Rogers had made nine films together and become *the* dancing team of the movies, Ginger decided to alter her course and take to dramatic roles. When Astaire signed to make a film for MGM, his first for that studio, the obvious solution was to co-star him with contractee Eleanor Powell, the number-one girl dancer of Hollywood. The result was *Broadway Melody of 1940*, notable for its Cole Porter score and a great amount of dancing but for little else.

George Murphy, who had danced with Powell in *Broadway Melody of 1938*, appeared here as a glib, conceited dancing star who accepts but doesn't appreciate the help of his partner. The pair break up when Murphy is offered the lead in a Broadway show starring Powell, but it is Astaire, modest and unselfish, who devises the dance routines and coaches Murphy.

Success goes to Murphy's head, and he alienates the people with whom he works. He turns up late and drunk one evening, and Astaire goes on in his place and does the opening number in mask and costume. The critics praise the costume number, which causes the ungrateful Murphy to become more conceited and Astaire to leave him. Powell, now in love with Astaire, points out to Murphy his stupid behavior, and he sees the light. Later he feigns drunkenness in order to cause Astaire to take over the show and receive the credit and applause he deserves. Then, his sense of decency restored, he joins them in the finale.

Of the Cole Porter songs, "I've Got My Eyes on You" and "I Concentrate on You" became popular in their own right. But the finale of the film, its most impressive part, used a song Porter had written in 1935, "Begin the Beguine." Here the marvelous melody is varied to allow for a dazzling choreographic production, with the stars dancing various styles to rhythms ranging from sultry to jazzy. The number runs a somewhat excessive six minutes, but it does give dance enthusiasts ample enjoyment in watching this one and only teaming of Fred Astaire and Eleanor Powell. Possibly it later occurred to all concerned that the dynamic Miss Powell was too good to be anybody's partner.

Fred Astaire, George Murphy and Eleanor Powell.

Joan Fontaine and Laurence Olivier.

Rebecca

1940

A Selznick International Production, released by United Artists; produced by David O. Selznick; directed by Alfred Hitchcock; screenplay by Robert E. Sherwood and Joan Harrison, based on the novel by Daphne du Maurier, adapted by Philip MacDonald and Michael Hogan; photographed by George Barnes; musical score by Franz Waxman; running time, 130 minutes.

Cast: Laurence Olivier (*Maxim de Winter*), Joan Fontaine (*Mrs. de Winter*), George Sanders (*Jack Favell*), Judith Anderson (*Mrs. Danvers*), Nigel Bruce (*Giles Lacy*), C. Aubrey Smith (*Colonel Julyan*), Reginald Denny (*Frank Crawley*), Gladys Cooper (*Beatrice Lacy*), Philip Winter (*Robert*), Edward Fielding (*Frith*), Florence Bates (*Mrs. Van Hopper*), Melville Cooper (*Coroner*), Leo G. Carroll (*Doctor Baker*), Forrester Harvey (*Chalcroft*), Lumsden Hare (*Tabbs*), Leonard Carey (*Ben*).

As had been the case with *Gone with the Wind* (1939), the leading female role in David O. Selz-

nick's *Rebecca* was much sought after. A number of famous actresses were tested, but Selznick settled for Joan Fontaine, then twenty-two and, despite having appeared in a dozen films, not looked upon as a star-caliber actress. Both director Alfred Hitchcock and co-star Laurence Olivier advised Selznick against using Fontaine. Olivier was eager to have his intended bride, Vivien Leigh, playing opposite him, and in view of her success as Scarlett O'Hara, Hollywood was amazed when Selznick decided that she was not quite right for the part.

Once *Rebecca* was completed and shown, it became obvious that Selznick knew his business—Fontaine was perfect as the gentle, timid girl who becomes the second Mrs. de Winter and gradually gains confidence as the wife of the lordly but tormented Maxim in a vast mansion apparently dominated by the memory of Maxim's deceased first wife, Rebecca.

Hitchcock arrived in Hollywood in 1939 to direct *Rebecca,* having gained an international reputation in his native England for making films marked with chilling suspense. With this film his fame ballooned. *Rebecca* is a magnificently produced picture. George Barnes's moody photography, Franz Waxman's eerie and romantic score, and Hitchcock's subtle pacing make a perfect framework for the acting of an almost all-British cast. Particularly memorable are the performances of George Sanders and Judith Anderson—the suave Sanders, with a voice like a supercilious cello, as a blackmailing cad and Anderson as Mrs. Danvers, the housekeeper of Manderley, a malicious woman devoted to her past mistress and bent on destroying the new one.

The spirit of Daphne du Maurier's novel was ably captured by the Selznick team, even though it was considered necessary to make a few changes, the main one being the manner in which Rebecca dies. Although she is set up at the start as a paragon of virtue, it becomes apparent that she was anything but. In the book she is killed by Maxim and her body placed on his yacht, which is then sunk. Selznick considered it wiser, in terms of gaining sympathy for the screen hero, to have her die accidentally but for the corpse to be disposed of in the same manner. When Manderly catches fire and burns to the ground, with the demented Mrs. Danvers perishing in the flames; the second Mrs. de Winter is finally rid of the influence of the vicious, amoral Rebecca.

As a film of wit, romance, and intriguing atmosphere, *Rebecca* is in a class of its own.

Joan Fontaine and Judith Anderson.

George Sanders, Joan Fontaine and Judith Anderson.

Laurence Olivier, Reginald Denny, Joan Fontaine, C. Aubrey Smith and George Sanders.

9

Waterloo Bridge

1940

An MGM Production; produced by Sidney Franklin; directed by Mervyn LeRoy; screenplay by S. N. Behrman, Hans Rameau, and George Froeschel, based on the play by Robert E. Sherwood; photographed by Joseph Ruttenberg; musical score by Herbert Stothart; running time, 103 minutes.

Cast: Vivien Leigh (*Myra*), Robert Taylor (*Roy Cronin*), Lucille Watson (*Lady Margaret Cronin*), Virginia Field (*Kitty*), Maria Ouspenskaya (*Olga Kirowa*), C. Aubrey Smith (*the Duke*), Janet Shaw (*Maureen*), Janet Waldo (*Elsa*), Steffi Duna (*Lydia*), Virginia Carroll (*Sylvia*), Leda Nicova (*Marie*), Florence Baker (*Beatrice*), Margery Manning (*Mary*), Frances MacInerney (*Violet*), Eleanor Stewart (*Grace*).

With husband-to-be Laurence Olivier working in Hollywood, Vivien Leigh remained on the scene and accepted an offer from MGM to star in *Waterloo Bridge*, her first picture after her enormous success in *Gone with the Wind*. Robert Taylor, very

handsome and adored by legions of female fans, was considered perfect casting opposite Leigh. Both stars readily agreed to the teaming, having become friends while making *A Yank at Oxford* two years previously in England.

Their vehicle was a heavily sentimental yarn about the vagaries of wartime romance that Metro had filmed in 1931 with Mae Clarke. The original material, a play by Robert E. Sherwood, was a rather doleful account of a Canadian soldier who falls in love with a prostitute in London during the First World War. The 1940 version was considerably laundered and lightened. Here the girl is a fragile and innocent young ballet dancer and the hero is an aristocratic British army officer. They meet in a fog on London's Waterloo Bridge and fall deeply in love. Their romance is sublime, and they soon agree to marry.

Waterloo Bridge is soap opera by experts. It was calculated to bring forth hankerchiefs in darkened theaters, and even those unaffected by its sentiment note the skill with which the picture was made. Herbert Stothart's musical scoring always leaned

10

Maria Ouspenskaya, Vivien Leigh and Virgina Field.

Robert Taylor, Vivien Leigh and C. Aubrey Smith.

heavily on muted violins, which was perfect in this instance. Mervyn LeRoy cunningly directed his players so that the audience was swept up by their joy and crushed by their tragedy.

The story is simple, although none too credible. The lovers' marriage has to be postponed when he is suddenly called to the front. Eventually she hears that he has been killed, and she becomes so distraught that she loses interest in dancing and in her dejection takes to the streets and becomes a prostitute. The hero returns, having been inaccurately listed as dead, and even though he wants to take her back and resume their life together, she considers herself now unfit. She commits suicide.

Robert Taylor claimed *Waterloo Bridge* as his favorite among his own films. He had not been much acclaimed as an actor, but he believed that this performance helped him establish his ability. However, Taylor always made a point of placing the success of the film in the lap of Vivien Leigh. The appeal, subtlety, and conviction of her performance give the otherwise doubtful yarn a true fascination.

Laurence Olivier and Greer Garson.

Pride and Prejudice

1940

An MGM Production; produced by Hunt Stromberg; directed by Robert Z. Leonard; screenplay by Aldous Huxley and Jane Murfin, based on the dramatization by Helen Jerome of the novel by Jane Austen; photographed by Karl Freund; musical score by Herbert Stothart; running time, 118 minutes.

Cast: Greer Garson (*Elizabeth Bennet*), Laurence Olivier (*Mr. Darcy*), Mary Boland (*Mrs. Bennet*), Edna May Oliver (*Lady Catherine de Bourgh*), Maureen O'Sullivan (*Jane Bennet*), Ann Rutherford (*Lydia Bennet*), Frieda Inescourt (*Miss Bingley*), Edmund Gwenn (*Mr. Bennet*), Karen Morley (*Charlotte Lucas*), Heather Angel (*Kitty Bennet*), Marsha Hunt (*Mary Bennet*), Bruce Lester (*Mr. Bingley*), Edward Ashley (*Mr. Wickham*), Melville Cooper (*Mr. Collins*), Marten Lamont (*Mr. Denny*), E. E. Clive (*Sir William Lucas*), May Beatty (*Mrs. Phillips*), Marjorie Wood (*Lady Lucas*).

It was once possible to make films about England in Hollywood. Because of a large and interesting resident colony of British actors, the studios could make a film like *Pride and Prejudice* with almost as much authenticity as if it had been done in London. This version of Jane Austen's novel of romance and social mores in early-nineteenth-century England had the advantages of a script written by the prestigious Aldous Huxley, in collaboration with Jane Murfin, and the presence of Laurence Olivier in the role of the proud and arrogant gentleman Mr. Darcey.

Olivier again wanted Vivien Leigh as his co-star, but MGM gave the role of Elizabeth Bennet, a lady of commanding beauty and intelligence, to Greer Garson, herself a lady of commanding beauty and intelligence. The previous year Garson had made a strong impression in her first film, playing the wife in *Goodbye Mr. Chips,* and she was clearly destined to be a star. It took her only another two years to win an Oscar, for symbolizing the courage of British women as *Mrs. Miniver.*

The Huxley treatment simplified the Austen comedy of manners. The film is basically the story of a modest middle-class family, the Bennets, whose mother (Mary Boland) is bent on finding husbands for her five daughters and whose father (Edmund

Gwenn) is forever embarrassed by the mother's antics. The eldest daughter, Elizabeth, is firm minded enough not to need help.

When the wealthy Darcy comes to live in their village the Bennet cap is set for him. This haughty fellow breaks up the romance between his friend Mr. Bingley (Bruce Lester) and Jane Bennet (Maureen O'Sullivan) because he considers the family beneath Bingley's station. Darcy's pride is almost his undoing. He falls in love with Elizabeth, but his actions have caused her to be prejudiced against him. It takes actions of other kinds before he can redeem himself in her eyes and win her hand.

Pride and Prejudice bubbles with humor and charm and style. The production values are faultless and the acting delightful. Olivier added to his popularity with this picture (it followed *Wuthering Heights* [1939] and *Rebecca)* and then made *That Hamilton Woman* with Vivien Leigh, whom he married just before that film went into production. They returned to England in December 1940, having completed a two-year period in Hollywood that had benefited both their careers.

Bruce Lester, Greer Garson, Frieda Inescourt and Laurence Olivier.

Maureen O'Sullivan, Mary Boland, Greer Garson and Edmund Gwenn.

Greer Garson, Edward Ashley, Laurence Olivier and E. E. Clive.

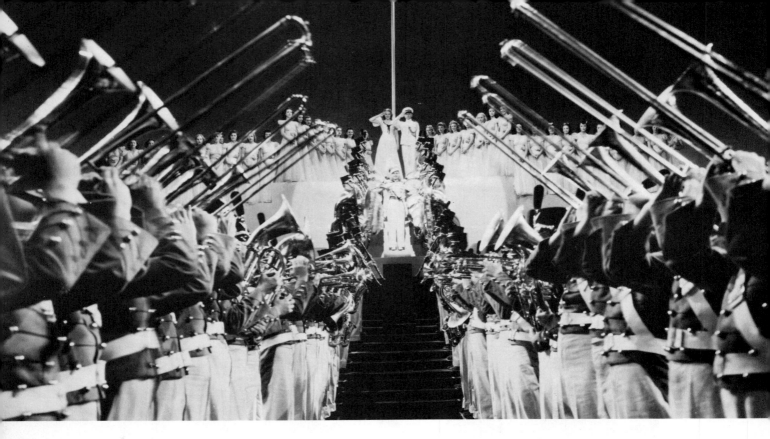

Strike Up the Band

1940

An MGM Production; produced by Arthur Freed; directed by Busby Berkeley; screenplay by John Monks, Jr., and Fred Finkelhoffe; photographed by Ray June; musical direction by George Stoll; running time, 119 minutes.

Cast: Mickey Rooney (*Jimmy Connors*), Judy Garland (*Mary Holden*), Paul Whiteman (*himself*), June Preisser (*Barbara Frances Morgan*), William Tracy (*Phillip Turner*), Larry Nunn (*Willie Brewster*), Margaret Early (*Annie*), Ann Shoemaker (*Mrs. Connors*), Francis Pierlot (*Mr. Judd*), Virginia Brissac (*Mrs. May Holden*), George Lessey (*Mr. Morgan*), Enid Bennett (*Mrs. Morgan*), Howard Hickman (*Doctor*), Sarah Edwards (*Miss Hodges*).

Mickey Rooney was declared the top star in the 1939 and 1940 popularity polls conducted by U.S. theater owners. By 1939 he had made several appearances as Andy Hardy, won a special Oscar for his dramatic work in *Boys Town* (1938), and co-starred with Judy Garland in *Babes in Arms* (1939). The latter had done so well that a sequel was mandatory. Again the director was Busby Berkeley, and the result was *Strike up the Band*, yet another showcase for the multitalented, stunningly energetic Rooney and the appealing, sweet-voiced Judy.

MGM's *Strike up the Band* bears no resemblance to the Gershwin stage musical except that it uses the spirited title for its finale. It's a smalltown story about musically ambitious college kids hoping to enter their swing band in a contest sponsored by Paul Whiteman. Bandleader Rooney and his chums lack the cash to get to the contest in Chicago, but by a great coincidence of the kind found only in movies like this, Whiteman and his band turn up in town to play a date. During a break in the session, when the Whiteman musicians leave the bandstand, Rooney and his group wander in to stare in admiration at the instruments. The temptation becomes too strong, and they start playing. They play so well that Whiteman stakes them to the money they need to get to Chicago. After plot complications (familial obligations and amorous misunderstandings) necessary to spin the picture out to two hours, the Rooney group wins the top prize.

Busby Berkeley did so well with Rooney and Garland that they did *Babes on Broadway* the following year. His musical routines were less lavish and geometric than they had been for Warners, but *Strike up the Band* is still marked by obvious Berkeley touches. Of particular note are "Do the Conga," which is a lengthy *perpetuum mobile* of amazing vitality, and a sequence in which Rooney maps out his band positions with pieces of fruit. He begins to conduct, and in his imagination the fruit becomes animated and performs as an orchestra.

Rooney, an excellent musician, appears to advantage in "Drummer Boy," and he and Garland perform an amusing vaudeville routine. Garland also made a lasting impression singing "Our Love Affair."

Strike up the Band is lightweight material, but for those who were youngsters when Rooney and Garland were youngsters, it is a film of considerable nostalgia.

In the foreground — Bill Tracy, Larry Nunn, Judy Garland, Mickey Rooney, Dick Paxton and Leonard Sues.

Paul Whiteman and Mickey Rooney.

Robert Cummings and Deanna Durbin.

Spring Parade

1940

A Universal Production; produced by Joe Pasternak; directed by Henry Koster; screenplay by Bruce Manning and Felix Jackson, based on a story by Ernst Marischka; photographed by Joseph Valentine; music by Robert Stolz, with lyrics by Gus Kahn; musical direction by Charles Previn; running time, 89 minutes.

Cast: Deanna Durbin (*Ilonka Tolnay*), Robert Cummings (*Harry Marten*), Mischa Auer (*the Peasant*), Henry Stephenson (*the Emperor*), S. Z. Sakall (*the Baker*), Butch and Buddy (*the Kids*), Walter Catlett (*Headwaiter*), Anne Gwynne (*Jenny*), Allyn Joslyn (*Count Zorndorf*), Peggy Moran (*Irene*), Reginald Denny (*Captain*), Franklin Pangborn (*Wiedelmeyer*), Ed Gargan (*Fortune-teller*), Samuel S. Hinds (*Von Zibberl*).

In 1936 fifteen-year-old Deanna Durbin starred in *Three Smart Girls* and won immediate popularity with her sparkling personality and her strong, beautifully toned singing voice. She followed it with six equally popular pictures that helped turn Universal from a shaky minor studio into a budding major one.

In 1940 came *Spring Parade,* a film of great charm and appeal and extraordinary in that it is an almost genuine Viennese operetta. The music was composed by Vienna's Robert Stolz, who had elected to leave Hitler's empire. For this happy enterprise he supplied, with lyrics by Gus Kahn, the rollicking "It's Foolish but It's Fun" and two waltz songs, "When April Sings" and "Waltzing in the Clouds." Durbin recorded all these for Decca.

Previously, Deanna Durbin had always appeared as a vivacious all-American girl. This time she plays a Hungarian peasant who travels to the Austrian capital to attend a carnival, where a fortune-teller informs her that she will marry an artist and receive help from a person of high rank.

She is befriended and employed by a kindly old baker, played by S. Z. Sakall, who had only recently arrived in Hollywood from Europe, in the delightfully befuddled style that would soon become familiar. He portrays a kind of flour-covered Santa Claus

S. Z. Sakall and Deanna Durbin.

Samuel S. Hinds, Anne Gwynne, Deanna Durbin and S. Z. Sakall.

Henry Stephenson, Deanna Durbin and S. Z. Sakall.

under whose friendly roof Deanna meets and falls for a handsome young army musician (Robert Cummings) with ambitions to become a composer.

Army regulations thwart this ambition, but Deanna circumnavigates all obstacles by appealing directly to dear old Emperor Franz Josef, played by dear old Henry Stephenson. Since Sakall supplies baked goods directly to the Court, Deanna slips a note into a bread stick bound for the emperor. The understanding monarch is amused by the appeal and orders the musician to appear at the next ball, to conduct the orchestra in his waltz and accompany his silver-throated girlfriend.

Since *Spring Parade* is total fantasy it requires no defense. It requires only a liking for the genial absurdity of Viennese operetta and an appreciation for Deanna Durbin at the crest of her young appeal. It became difficult for Universal to find suitable vehicles to continue marketing that appeal, and by 1947, after starring in twenty-one films, she decided to terminate her career. Deanna's pretty face and pure soprano are among the most pleasant memories of moviegoing in the forties.

Cary Grant and Katharine Hepburn.

The Philadelphia Story

1940

An MGM Production; produced by Joseph L. Mankiewicz; directed by George Cukor; screenplay by Donald Ogden Stewart, based on the play by Philip Barry; photographed by Joseph Ruttenberg; musical score by Franz Waxman; running time, 112 minutes.

Cast: Cary Grant (*C. K. Dexter Haven*), Katharine Hepburn (*Tracy Lord*), James Stewart (*Mike Connor*), Ruth Hussey (*Liz Imbrey*), John Howard (*George Kittredge*), Ronald Young (*Uncle Willie*), John Halliday (*Seth Lord*), Virginia Weidler (*Dinah Lord*), Mary Nash (*Margaret Lord*), Henry Daniell (*Sidney Kidd*), Lionel Pape (*Edward*), Rex Evans (*Thomas*), Russ Clark (*John*), Hilda Plowright (*Librarian*), Lita Chevret (*Manicurist*), Lee Phelps (*Bartender*).

The triumph of *The Philadelphia Story* is very largely the triumph of Katharine Hepburn, one of the most forceful, strong-minded women Hollywood has ever known. She had arrived in California in 1932, at twenty-five, following a short career on the stage, and co-starred with John Barrymore in *Bill of Divorcement*. During the next six years she made fourteen more films, and although they gave her a good reputation as an actress with a distinct personality, she found her popularity slipping and her future doubtful.

Wisely, she withdrew from Hollywood and

20

Katharine Hepburn and James Stewart.

Katharine Hepburn, Cary Grant, Mary Nash, John
Halliday, James Stewart and Ruth Hussey.

Cary Grant and James Stewart.

returned to New York to look for a good stage
property. In Philip Barry she discovered a playwright with an interesting outline for a play. She
persuaded him to complete it, with her in mind as
the lead, and together they took it to the Theatre
Guild and offered to put up half the money for the
production. The play opened in March 1939 and
brought Hepburn great attention and approval.

In seeking the film rights, Hollywood found the
principal owner to be Miss Hepburn, who drove a
hard bargain—whoever made the film would have
to acquire her along with the rights, and she would
have director and co-star approval. MGM made the
best offer, a quarter of a million dollars for property and stars. They agreed to George Cukor as
director and to Cary Grant as C. K. Dexter Haven,
the playboyish ex-husband of beautiful but haughty
and self-willed Tracy Lord.

In playing Tracy Lord, Hepburn not only had
the advantage of knowing every line and nuance
from hundreds of stage performances, but she also
understood the kind of woman she was playing.
Herself a New Englander of prominent family,
complete with Byrn Mawr education, she knew the
mannerisms and life-style of the Philadelphia aristo-
crats.

The beauty of this witty adult comedy is its
"taming of the shrew" theme of an arrogant woman
humanized by love. This is achieved by the concern
of two men—Dexter, who still loves her and doesn't
want to see her get married to a stuffy blueblood,
and a warmhearted newspaperman, played by
James Stewart, assigned to cover the marriage.
Unimpressed by wealth, the reporter spots the soft-
ness under Tracy's charmingly brash exterior. He
falls in love with her, and she with him, but in the
end he comes to realize that her place is with
Dexter. The fear expressed by her father, that she
has everything but an understanding heart, proves
groundless.

The Philadelphia Story is a product of the
Golden Age of Movie Comedy. It is elegant, stylish,
quickwitted, and genuinely funny in its understanding of human foibles. Its three stars went on to even
greater popularity, each of them unique.

James Stewart won an *Oscar* for his performance
in *The Philadelphia Story*, and Donald Ogden
Stewart received one for his screenplay.

Sixteen years later MGM pulled out the script
and produced a musical version with Grace Kelly,
Bing Crosby, and Frank Sinatra. The result was
pleasant enough, thanks to songs by Cole Porter,
but it lacked the incisive humor of the original.

Basil Rathbone and Tyrone Power.

The Mark of Zorro

1940

A 20th Century-Fox Production; produced by Raymond Griffith; directed by Rouben Mamoulian: screenplay by John Tainton Foote, adapted by Garrett Fort and Bess Meredyth from the novel *The Curse of Capistrano*, by Johnston McCulley; photographed by Arthur Miller; musical score by Alfred Newman; running time, 93 minutes.

Cast: Tyrone Power (*Diego*), Linda Darnell (*Lolita Quintero*), Basil Rathbone (*Captain Esteban Pasquale*), Gale Sondergaard (*Inez Quintero*), Eugene Pallette (*Father Felipe*), J. Edward Bromberg (*Don Luis Quintero*), Montagu Love (*Don Alejandro Vega*), Janet Beecher (*Señora Isabella Vega*), Robert Lowery (*Rodrigo*), Chris-Pin Martin (*Turnkey*), George Regas (*Sergeant Gonzales*), Belle Mitchell (*Maria*), John Bleifer (*Pedro*), Frank Puglia (*Café Proprietor*), Eugen Borden (*Officer of the Day*), Pedro de Cordoba (*Don Miguel*).

The inevitable comparison of this film with the Douglas Fairbanks, Sr., production of 1921 is double edged. There is, of course, no comparison at all between the physical performances of Tyrone Power and the incredibly athletic Fairbanks. On the other hand the Fairbanks version can't hold a candle to the elegant production values of this one.

Rouben Mamoulian's pictures were always marked by his artistic taste, and *The Mark of Zorro* is a triumph of his style. He had the advantage of a photographer, Arthur Miller, whose black-and-white images were so crisp and so well lit that they suggested color, and a musical score by Alfred Newman that matched Mamoulian's brisk pacing.

Tyrone Power, handsome, personable, and a much better actor than credited at the time, perfectly suggested the role of the hero, but his swashbuckling was actually contrived by Mamoulian's cunning editing and doubling.

Loosely based on an episode of Spanish-Califor-

Basil Rathbone, Belle Mitchell, Gale Sondergaard, J. Edward Bromberg, Linda Darnell and Tyrone Power.

nia history (circa 1820), the story tells of a son's returning to Los Angeles after completing his education at a Spanish military academy, to find his father deposed as governor and a buffoon (J. Edward Bromberg) in his place. The new governor is really a pawn in the hands of his military advisor —Basil Rathbone at his darkly villainous best.

To solve the situation the young man gives the impression of being a fop, to the disgust of his family and the disdain of the girl to whom he is attracted, the governor's niece (Linda Darnell). But at night he dons a mask and a black costume, terrifies the governor, gives Rathbone concern, wins the admiration of the niece, and with his sword scatches the letter *Z* all over the place.

The film's inevitable conclusion finds him liquidating the rotten element, winning the girl, and regaining his father's esteem. But predictable as it is, it is done with panache.

This *Zorro* is among the finest examples of its genre, and one of its great assets is Basil Rathbone. Biting his dialogue with perfect diction and bristling with malevolence, Rathbone here played brilliantly. He was among the few actors who really excelled at swordplay, and he could easily have bested any of the heroes to whom he was forced to lose. The duel in this film, with Albert Cavens doubling for Power in the long shots, rates high in the far-from-crowded category of good film swordplay.

Linda Darnell and Tyrone Power.

Tyrone Power and Basil Rathbone.

Ginger Rogers and Ernest Cossart.

James Craig and Ginger Rogers.

Kitty Foyle

1940

An RKO-Radio Production; produced by David Hempstead; directed by Sam Wood; screenplay by Dalton Trumbo, with additional dialogue by Donald Ogden Stewart, based on the novel by Christopher Morley; photographed by Robert De Grasse; musical score by Roy Webb; running time, 107 minutes.

Cast: Ginger Rogers (*Kitty Foyle*), Dennis Morgan (*Wyn Strafford*), James Craig (*Dr. Mark Eljen*), Eduardo Ciannelli (*Giono*), Ernest Cossart (*Pop*), Gladys Cooper (*Mrs. Strafford*), Odette Myrtil (*Delphine Detafile*), Mary Treen (*Pat*), Katherine Stevens (*Molly*), Walter Kingsford (*Mr. Kennett*), Cecil Cunningham (*Grandmother*), Nella Walker (*Aunt Jessica*), Edward Fielding (*Uncle Edgar*), Kay Linaker (*Wyn's Wife*), Richard Nichols (*Wyn's Boy*), Florence Bates (*Customer*).

The impression that Ginger Rogers won an Oscar as a dramatic actress the moment she stopped being Fred Astaire's dancing partner is more than a little exaggerated. She had begun her Hollywood career in 1930, at nineteen, and she had played in forty films by the time she made *Kitty Foyle*. Her ninth picture with Astaire, *The Story of Irene and Vernon Castle,* was followed by leads in four light comedies. Then came *Kitty Foyle*, the first major dramatic feature in which she was the only star.

Whether viewed in 1940 or today, the film has little to recommend it other than Rogers' performance. This was a pulp-magazine soap opera, although from the pen of the reputable Christopher Morley. Its heroine is a Philadelphia working-class girl who painfully dallies with the upper social stratum but settles for a more comfortable milieu. Dalton Trumbo's screenplay veered away from Morley's social commentary and stressed the emotional aspects of the tale.

Sam Wood used stream of consciousness in directing the heroine's recollections. Alone in her bedroom, Kitty looks at her reflection in the mirror, and the image becomes an alter ego. From her discourse with the image comes the story of Kitty, daughter of a respectable working man but dreaming of one day living on a higher level. On the eve of her marriage to Dr. Mark Eljen (James Craig), she meets an old flame, Wyn Strafford (Dennis Morgan), a charming blade from a Main Line family. Against the wishes of his family they marry, but she grows disenchanted with his lack of character and leaves him. Kitty bears his child, but it is stillborn and she decides not to tell him. After much soul searching she returns to the arms of the everfaithful doctor. Thus the picture, which was deliberately intended as a "woman's picture," has a "sensible" ending.

Kitty Foyle needed the no-nonsense guiding hand of Sam Wood and the skill of Ginger Rogers to save it from slipping into sentimental slush. She showed genuine surprise when declared Best Actress of 1940, with good reason. The competition was Bette Davis in *The Letter,* Joan Fontaine in *Rebecca*, Martha Scott in *Our Town*, and Katharine Hepburn in *The Philadelphia Story.*

Ginger Rogers and Dennis Morgan.

Ernest Cossart, Ginger Rogers and Dennis Morgan.

Walter Brennan, Gary Cooper, Irving Bacon, Barbara Stanwyck and James Gleason.

Meet John Doe

1941

A Warner Bros. Production; produced and directed by Frank Capra; screenplay by Robert Riskin; photographed by George Barnes; musical score by Dimitri Tiomkin; running time, 123 minutes.

Cast: Gary Cooper (*Long John Willoughby*), Barbara Stanwyck (*Ann Mitchell*), D. B. Norton (*Edward Arnold*), Walter Brennan *(Colonel)*, James Gleason (*Henry Connell*), Spring Byington *(Mrs. Mitchell)*, Gene Lockhart (*Mayor*), Rod La Rocque *(Ted Sheldon)*, Irving Bacon (*Beanny*), Regis Toomey (*Bert Hansen*), Warren Hymer *(Angelface)*, Aldrich Bowker (*Pop Dwyer*), Ann Doran *(Mrs. Hansen)*, Sterling Holloway *(Dan)*, Mrs. Gardner Grane *(Mrs. Brewster)*, J. Farrell MacDonald (*Sourpuss Smithers*). Pat Flaherty *(Mike.)*

The combination of Gary Cooper and Frank Capra was perfectly natural. Cooper was a universal idealization of the American male, and Capra specialized in Americana. In 1936 Cooper had appeared in Capra's *Mr. Deeds Goes to Town*, playing an honest, naïve smalltown fellow who inherits a fortune and decides to give it all away. In 1940, when Capra and scenarist Robert Riskin came across a story about a simple American running afoul of fascism, they considered only one actor for the part. Cooper agreed to play it even before Riskin had written the script.

Meet John Doe was clearly a picture with a message. Hitler's success had given certain Americans with fascistic leanings confidence that some kind of New Order was possible in the United States. Capra aimed to point this out to the millions of moviegoers, the "John Does," and he succeeded.

Cooper appeared here not only as a common man, but as one down on his luck—a baseball player who, because of an arm injury, has had to give up the game and become a hobo. A tough-minded newspaperwoman (Barbara Stanwyck),

Standing — Rod La Roque, Gary Cooper, Edward Arnold and Barbara Stanwyck.

JOHN DOE
Sponsored by
THE NEW BULLETIN

fired from her job, writes a story in her final column to express her contempt for management and business ethics. She invents a man named John Doe and quotes him as saying that he will commit suicide on Christmas Eve as a protest against greed and hypocrisy.

To avoid appearing ridiculous to its rivals, her newspaper rehires her and tells her to find a man to play the person she has invented. She discovers the destitute, hungry ex-ballplayer and talks him into assuming the role.

As John Doe he becomes a beloved national figure, as he delivers columns and speeches, written for him by Stanwyck, on the need for love, decency, and understanding among all peoples. John Doe clubs spring up all over the country, and a power-ful, politically ambitious publisher (Edward Arnold) spots this as an opportunity to further his third party. He organizes a huge rally and nominates John Doe as his presidential candidate.

Doe refuses, and the angry publisher then exposes him as a fake. To avoid disillusioning his public, he decides to prove his sincerity by committing suicide, as specified in the original letter. But before he can leap to his death from a high tower the reporter stops him—and tells him she loves and wants him.

Only the ending of *Meet John Doe* rings false, but after five different attempts Capra and Riskin admitted that it was the best they could do. They can be forgiven. Most of the film, and every minute of the acting, is superb.

Barbara Stanwyck and Gary Cooper.

Edward G. Robinson.

The Sea Wolf

1941

A Warner Bros. Production; produced by Hal B. Wallis; directed by Michael Curtiz; screenplay by Robert Rossen, based on the novel by Jack London; photographed by Sol Polito; musical score by Erich Wolfgang Korngold; running time, 100 minutes.

Cast: Edward G. Robinson (*Wolf Larsen*), John Garfield (*George Leach*), Ida Lupino (*Ruth Webster*), Alexander Knox (*Humphrey Van Weydon*), Gene Lockhart (*Dr. Louie Prescott*), Barry Fitzgerald (*Cooky*), Stanley Ridges (*Johnson*), Francis McDonald (*Svensen*), David Bruce (*Young Sailor*), Howard da Silva (*Smoke*), Frank Lackteen (*Agent*), Charles Sullivan (*First Mate*), Ernie Adams (*pickpocket*), Jeane Cowan (*Singer*).

Jack London's adventure stories are natural for screen treatment, and *The Sea Wolf* has been filmed six times. By far the best version is the one directed by Michael Curtiz for Warners in 1941, starring Edward G. Robinson as Wolf Larsen, the satanic captain of the scavenger ship *Ghost*. The literate script by Robert Rossen accented the character of Larsen, showing him as a subtly evil, treacherous, mentally unstable tyrant and a thwarted intellectual who has studied poetry and philosophy in his lonely privacy.

The film allowed Robinson something he richly deserved but seldom got—top billing and a major characterization. In this he was splendidly backed by the resources of Warners, utilizing a huge studio tank and their newly installed fog machines. The film is shrouded in fog from start to finish, cleverly photographed in low key by Sol Polito and matched by the subdued, eerie musical score of Erich Wolfgang Korngold.

Rossen added a character to the London story, the part of a young drifter who signs on the *Ghost* —the rest of the crew had to be shanghaied—to elude the police. The part was created for John Garfield and also gave a sadly romantic counterpoint for Ida Lupino's role as a drab and sickly girl who is picked up in the night fog of San Francisco harbor when the ferry she is riding is sunk in an accident.

Picked up at the same time is scholarly gentleman named Humphrey Van Weydon, beautifully played by Alexander Knox in his first Hollywood film. The Canadian actor had recently arrived from the London stage. Van Weydon is forced to work as a servant, but his quiet, civilized presence gradually unsettles Larsen and brings about his end.

Larsen goes blind, and when he can no longer hide this from his servile crew they leave the ship. To allow Garfield and Lupino to escape, Van Weydon sacrifices his own life, staying with the stricken captain as the *Ghost* sinks.

Robinson's Larsen is spiritually related to Captain Ahab, and his acting develops the role fully. Fully developed also are such minor roles as the drunken ship's doctor who kills himself rather than suffer any more of Larsen's humiliation, played by Gene Lockhart, and the malicious cook, played by Barry Fitzgerald. In its performances and its somber, mysterious atmosphere *The Sea Wolf* is a masterpiece.

Edward G. Robinson, John Garfield and Ida Lupino.

John Garfield and Edward G. Robinson.

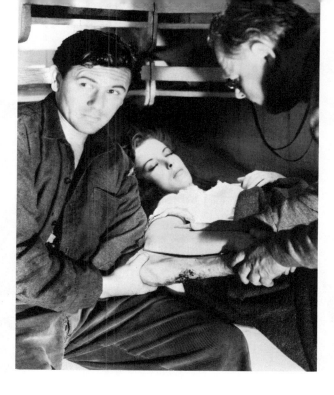

John Garfield, Ida Lupino and Gene Lockhart.

Edward G. Robinson and Alexander Knox.

Henry Fonda, William Demarest and Robert Greig.

Barbara Stanwyck and Henry Fonda.

The Lady Eve

Barbara Stanwyck, Henry Fonda and Eugene Pallette.

1941

A Paramount Production; produced by Paul Jones; directed and written by Preston Sturges, based on a story by Moncton Hale; photographed by Victor Milner; musical direction by Sigmund Krumgold; running time, 97 minutes.

Cast: Barbara Stanwyck (*Jean-Eve*), Henry Fonda (*Charles Pike*), Charles Coburn (*Colonel Harrington*), Eugene Pallette (*Mr. Pike*), William Demarest (*Muggsy*), Eric Blore (*Sir Alfred McGlennan Keith*), Melville Cooper (*Gerald*), Martha O'Driscoll (*Martha*), Janet Beecher (*Mrs. Pike*), Robert Greig (*Burrows*), Dora Clement (*Gertrude*), Luis Alberni (*Pike's Chef*).

Preston Sturges (1898–1959) was very much a figure of early-1940s films. He had been a successful writer at Paramount for some years when he finally persuaded the studio to let him direct his own material. In 1940 he made two small-budget pictures—*The Great McGinty*, a political satire, and *Christmas in July*, a spoof on the advertising business. Both were minor gems and profitable enough to get him a big budget and big names for his third venture.

The Lady Eve, with Henry Fonda and Barbara Stanwyck, is possibly his most brilliant film. It allowed Fonda a chance at comedy after too many parts in dull roles, and he performed with a skill that won him new fans. The picture gave the same needed opportunity to Stanwyck, who here played the slyest of sexy vamps.

This is a battle of the sexes, with woman very much the winner. Charles Pike (Fonda) is a rather dull young millionaire, innocent of guile, wary of women because he believes they want only his money, and devoted to a life of scientific exploration. Snakes are his area of study.

Returning to the United States on a luxury ocean liner, he is spotted by Jean (Stanwyck), who travels in the company of her father (Charles Coburn) and makes a living as a cardsharp. She and her father ply the luxury lines bilking the wealthy. Jean first gets Pike's attention by tripping him, and then she uses all her talent to make him fall in love with her. The scheme is well underway when Pike's

tough and vigilant bodyguard (William Demarest) exposes Jean as having a police record. Pike wipes Jean out of his life.

She, however, is not about to give up. She now assumes another guise and appears in Pike's life as an English gentlewoman named Eve. The naïve millionaire again falls into the trap, little realizing that he is being put through an identical hoop. Jean is actually bent on revenge for being dumped the first time, so on their wedding night she starts to admit past errors and sins. The list grows and grows until Pike walks away in disgust.

Sometime later, on another ship, Jean again trips Pike as he passes. Again he falls into her arms, and this time he is glad to see her, sorry for past misunderstandings, and so thoroughly confused that he completely capitulates. "I don't want to understand," he says. "I don't wanna know. Whatever it is, keep it to yourself. All I know is I adore you. I'll never leave you again. We'll work it out somehow."

As a satire on the man-woman relationship, packed with quickly paced verbal and visual wit and populated with wacky but believable characters, *The Lady Eve* may never be equaled.

Eugene Pallette, Janet Beecher, Henry Fonda, Barbara Stanwyck and Eric Blore.

William Powell and Myrna Loy.

Love Crazy

William Powell, Gail Patrick, Myrna Loy and Jack Carson.

An MGM Production; produced by Pandro S. Berman; directed by Jack Conway; screenplay by William Ludwig, Charles Lederer, and David Hertz; photographed by Ray June; musical score by David Snell; running time, 100 minutes.

Cast: William Powell (*Steve Ireland*), Myrna Loy (*Susan Ireland*), Gail Patrick (*Isobel Grayson*), Jack Carson (*Ward Willoughby*), Florence Bates (*Mrs. Cooper*), Sidney Blackmer (*George Renny*), Sig Rumann (*Dr. Wuthering*), Vladimir Sokoloff (*Dr. Klugle*), Donald MacBride (*Pinky Grayson*), Sara Haden (*Cecilia Landis*), Fern Emmett (*Martha*), Joseph Crehan (*Judge*), Elisha Cook, Jr. (*Elevator Boy*).

William Powell and Myrna Loy appeared together in a dozen films, six of them as Mr. and Mrs. Nick Charles in the *Thin Man* series. Whether as Dashiel Hammett's detectives, as Mr. and Mrs. Flo Ziegfeld, or as any other married couple, their playing together was delightfully deft. Film fans looked upon them as the ideal pair, a lady and a gentleman—warm, humorous, and civilized and therefore very rare, in the movies and in life. In *Love Crazy* this "perfect celluloid marriage," as Hollywood called it, was put to the test for the sake of frantic comedy. Its success was due to Powell's great ability as a farceur. Miss Loy, ever cool and elegant, performed mostly as a foil.

The picture sets up Steve and Susan Ireland as a happy couple on the verge of celebrating their fourth wedding anniversary. Intimations of trouble arrive with Susan's mother (Florence Bates). She twists her ankle, and Steve looks after her while his wife meets an aunt. Bored with his charge, he wanders out of the apartment and happens to run into an old girlfriend (Gail Patrick), a meeting observed by mother-in-law.

Informed of this, Susan decides to call on the girl's husband, but she mistakenly gets into the wrong apartment and meets a vain archery champion (Jack Carson) who insists on demonstrating his skill. In retreating to the hall she is followed by the stripped-to-the-waist champ and runs into her husband.

The ensuing charges and counterchanges result in Susan's demanding a divorce. He agrees but later realizes that he loves Susan and doesn't want to lose her. Desperate for a way to negate her case, he seizes

Myrna Loy, William Powell and Florence Bates.

upon the fact that she cannot proceed if he is declared insane.

The bulk of *Love Crazy's* humor stems from William Powell's efforts to convince people that he is mad, which isn't as easy as he thinks. However, once he is registered as a lunatic he is carted off to a sanitarium, and he then has the problem of persuading people that he *isn't* insane. In order to escape he impersonates an elderly aunt, which brings on its own problems, all of which are eventually solved, to bring about the entente desired by the distraught husband—and the audience. It is nothing but delightful nonsense played in high style by a couple whose like is sorely missed.

William Powell, Myrna Loy and Sig Rumann.

Carole Landis, Robert Cummings and Betty Grable.

The Condos Brothers and Betty Grable.

Moon over Miami

1941

A 20th Century-Fox Production; produced by Harry Joe Brown; directed by Walter Lang; screenplay by Vincent Lawrence and Brown Holmes, based on a story by Stephen Powys, adapted by George Seaton; photographed in Technicolor by Peverell Marley and Leon Shamroy; songs by Leo Robin and Ralph Rainger; musical direction by Alfred Newman; running time, 91 minutes.

Cast: Don Ameche (*Phil O'Neil*), Betty Grable (*Kay*), Robert Cummings (*Jeff Bolton*), Charlotte Greenwood (*Aunt Susie*), Jack Haley (*Mike*), Carole Landis (*Barbara*), Cobina Wright, Jr. (*Connie*), George Lessey (*William Bolton*), Robert Conway (*Lester*), the Condos Brothers (*themselves*), Robert Greig (*Brearly*), Minor Watson (*Reynolds*), Fortunio Bonanova (*Mr. Pretto*), George Humbert (*Drive-in Boss*), Stephen Charters (*Postman*), Lynn Roberts (*Jennie May*), Larry McGrath (*Bartender*).

The late Betty Grable was a pleasant, modest lady who never claimed to be anything other than a

lightweight talent. She enjoyed her work and realized that it brought pleasure to a large audience, particularly World War II servicemen. She began in motion pictures as a fifteen-year-old in 1931 and did bit parts all through the thirties, but her career moved into high gear when she signed with 20th Century-Fox in 1939.

Wisely, she insisted on accepting a Broadway offer to play in Cole Porter's *DuBarry Was a Lady* before making a film on her new contract. Her Broadway success won the esteem she sought, and Fox then starred her in *Down Argentina Way*, the first of about twenty Fox-Grable Technicolor musicals.

After she co-starred with Alice Faye in *Tin Pan Alley*, the studio groomed her as a replacement for Faye, who had hinted that she was about to retire, and gave her top billing in *Moon over Miami*, a musical version of *Three Blind Mice*, which Fox had made with Loretta Young in 1938.

Moon over Miami is an agreeable item, if viewed purely for what it is—a celluloid candy. The plot tells of a pair of Texas sisters (Grable and Carole Landis) and their aunt (Charlotte Greenwood) who come into a small inheritance and decide to spend it on an expedition to Miami to land a couple of husbands among the wealthy set. They check into a lavish hotel, Grable posing as a rich girl, with Landis as her secretary and Greenwood as her maid. They soon receive the attention of a wealthy playboy (Robert Cummings) and formerly wealthy chum (Don Ameche). Everyone charms everyone else, and Grable lands Cummings, only to find that she loves Ameche, who doesn't think much of Grable because of her gold-digging. But Cummings discovers that it's Landis he really cares for, and when Grable admits the truth she wins Ameche.

The film affords some fleeting shots of a 1941 Miami, almost quaint in comparison to the large, garish city of today, and interesting location sequences of aquatic and underwater activities in Cypress Gardens and Silver Springs. Of the eight songs supplied by Leo Robin and Ralph Rainger two linger in the memory—"Oh Me, Oh Miami" and "You Started Something." Grable's singing was modest, but her dancing, particularly her tapdancing with the Condos Brothers, was very pleasing, as was all of the film.

Robert Cummings, Don Ameche and Betty Grable.

Charlotte Greenwood, Carole Landis, Betty Grable and Jack Haley.

Glenn Ford and William Holden.

Texas

1941

A Columbia Production; produced by Samuel Bischoff; directed by George Marshall; screenplay by Horace McCoy, Lewis Meltzer, and Michael Blankfort; photographed by George Meehan; musical score by Sidney Cutner; running time, 93 minutes.

Cast: William Holden (*Dan Thomas*), Glenn Ford (*Tod Ramsey*), Claire Trevor (*Mike King*), George Bancroft (*Windy Miller*), Edgar Buchanan (*Doc Thorpe*), Don Beddoe (*Sheriff*), Andrew Tombes (*Tennessee*), Addison Richards (*Matt Lasham*), Edmund MacDonald (*Comstock*), Joseph Crehan (*Dusty King*), Willard Robertson (*Wilson*), Patrick Moriarty (*Mathews*), Edmund Cobb (*Blaire*).

Although Westerns had been a staple product right from the beginning in Hollywood, not until the late thirties did the studios begin producing them in epic form, with star names and big budgets. These Westerns were for the general market, and they had little impact on the continual churning out of cheapie Westerns for the juvenile trade.

Columbia got into the act in 1940 by making *Arizona*, with Jean Arthur and William Holden, a somewhat ponderous tribute to pioneerism. They quickly realized that historical accuracy was not as profitable as fictional excitement and teamed Holden with Glenn Ford in *Texas*, a slam-bang piece of entertainment directed by George Marshall. Marshall's sense of humor had been apparent in two previous big Westerns, *Destry Rides Again* (1939) and *When the Daltons Rode* (1940), and *Texas* has an almost slapstick quality.

The setting is the Texas cattle country right after the Civil War. Two young roughnecks (Holden and Ford) drift into town and get into trouble. To save them from being jailed, Holden enters a boxing contest against the local champ, and the wildly comic match ends in a general street brawl. Later the two are mistaken for stagecoach bandits, but they manage to escape the posse and eventually drift apart.

The two heroes meet a few years later and find themselves aligned with opposing factions—Ford has settled down to ranching, but the rambunctious Holden is happily engaged as an outlaw, in a gang headed by the town dentist (Edgar Buchanan). Adding to their confusion is their competition for the affections of lovely Claire Trevor. The morality strictures of the Hays Office made the outcome obvious.

Texas is full of gunsmoke, fistfights, galloping horses, rampaging cattle, and amusingly absurd characters, all directed by Marshall at a dizzying pace. It was an excellent vehicle for Holden and Ford, two handsome young actors at the start of long and successful film careers. They teamed again in 1948 for another Western, *The Man from Colorado*, and separately made notable entries in this genre. *Texas* is also notable for giving Edgar Buchanan his first major part, launching him on his way to becoming a familiar movie character. Before he turned to acting Buchanan had been a dentist, and his scenes in this film as a crude practitioner of frontier dentistry have a painful humor to them.

Edgar Buchanan and William Holden.

Edgar Buchanan, Glenn Ford, William Holden and Claire Trevor.

Claire Trevor and William Holden.

41

Ian Hunter (Minister), Brian Aherne and Jeanette MacDonald.

Smilin' Through

1941

An MGM Production; produced by Victor Saville; directed by Frank Borzage; screenplay by Donald Ogden Stewart and John Balderston, based on the play by Jane Cowl and Jane Murfin; photographed in Technicolor by Leonard Smith; musical acore by Herbert Stothart; running time, 100 minutes.

Cast: Jeanette MacDonald (*Kathleen and Moonyean Clare*), Brian Aherne (*Sir John Carteret*), Gene Raymond (*Kenneth Wayne* and *Jeremy Wayne*), Ian Hunter, (*the Reverend Owen Harding*), Frances Robinson (*Ellen*), Patrick Moore (*Willie*), Eric Lonsdale (*Batman*), Jackie Horner (*Kathleen as a child*), David Clyde (*Sexton*).

To like this version of *Smilin' Through*, one must be fond of Jeanette MacDonald. Otherwise it becomes a very old-fashioned, oversentimental yarn of tragedy and romance. The stage play by Jane

Cowl and Jane Murfin had been filmed in 1922 with Norma Talmadge and in 1932 with Norma Shearer, and in refurbishing it as a MacDonald vehicle MGM added a few songs and gave it superb color photography. In any version it is not a film for realists.

The story requires its star to play dual roles. For most of the story she is a young Irish girl, Kathleen, who wants to marry a handsome young soldier about to march off to World War I but is prevented from it by her elderly English guardian (Brian Aherne with wrinkles and white hair). Forced to give an explanation, he tells her of Moonyean Claire, the lovely girl he almost married. A flashback tells the story for him: The young Aherne stands at the altar about to be joined in wedlock with Moonyean, when her handsome but insanely jealous suitor (Gene Raymond) enters and aims a pistol at Aherne. As Moonyean moves to stop him she receives the bullet in her heart and dies in the

42

arms of her intended husband. The suitor hastily departs for Canada.

Old Aherne's ward listens tearfully and then receives the really hard news—the boy she loves is the son of the murderous suitor (Gene Raymond also portrays the son, but with a happier demeanor). Kathleen is shaken by this revelation, but it doesn't alter her feelings for the boy.

He goes to war assured of her love and hoping that the guardian will relent. His strongest ally is the ghost of Moonyean, who convinces the old man that he should forgive the youngsters and allow them their love. He agrees, and when he dies the image of him as a young man rises from his old body and joins Moonyean. Together they look on with approval at Kathleen and her young man.

Smilin' Through is obviously a vehicle of another time, a refined tearjerker but certainly a good one. It marked the high point in Jeanette MacDonald's film career. She looked radiant in her late thirties and sang such old ballads as "A Little Love, A Little Kiss," "The Kerry Dance," the title song, and some ditties of the war period. This was also her only film with her husband Gene Raymond. She made only five more films, none of them very successful, and by the end of the forties retired from the screen.

Gene Raymond and Jeannette MacDonald.

Brian Aherne and Jeanette MacDonald.

Brian Aherne and Jeanette MacDonald.

Gene Raymond and Jeanette MacDonald.

Arthur Kennedy and Errol Flynn.

Errol Flynn and Olivia de Havilland.

They Died with Their Boots On

1941

A Warner Bros. Production; produced by Hal B. Wallis; directed by Raoul Walsh; screenplay by Wally Kline and Aeneas MacKenzie; photographed by Bert Glennon; musical score by Max Steiner; running time, 140 minutes.

Cast: Errol Flynn (*George Armstrong Custer*), Olivia de Havilland (*Elizabeth Bacon Custer*), Arthur Kennedy (*Ned Sharp*), Charley Grapewin (*California Joe*), Gene Lockhart (*Samuel Bacon*), Anthony Quinn (*Crazy Horse*), Stanley Ridges (*Major Romulus Taipe*), John Litel (*General Philip Sheridan*), Walter Hampden (*William Sharp*), Sydney Greenstreet (*General Winfield Scott*), Regis Toomey (*Fitzhugh Lee*), Hattie McDaniel (*Callie*), G. P. Huntley, Jr. (*Lieutenant Butler*), Frank Wilcox (*Captain Webb*), Joseph Sawyer (*Sergeant Doolittle*), Minor Watson (*Senator Smith*), Joseph Crehan (*President Grant*).

Errol Flynn was an excellent choice to play George Armstrong Custer. Both the actor and the soldier were handsome, cavalier figures and laws unto themselves. Lack of self-discipline undermined both their lives. This well-mounted and exciting account of Custer's career stays within a certain factual framwork, but it considerably alters its hero's intentions and attitudes.

Custer was not the paragon here depicted, but at the other extreme, neither was he the hysterical, cowardly idiot displayed in *Little Big Man* (1970). His brief career was marked by great personal bravery and some brilliance as a cavalry commander,

44

but he was also a vainglorious, selfish, ambitious man who lived to be only thirty-seven.

At the time of his death he was under suspended court martial. As part of a military campaign against the plains Indians he was instructed to make no move on his own volition; but he was so eager to make the campaign a personal victory, to clear himself of certain charges, and to win public favor so that he could run for president that he made the fatal blunder that has euphemistically gone down in history as his Last Stand. Despite overlooking this aspect of his career, *They Died with Their Boots On* presents a good characterization of Custer.

The film begins with his arrival at West Point, decked out in a lavish uniform in deference to his hero, Marshal Murat, Napoleon's brilliant cavalry tactician, and then paints him as wretchedly poor scholar but a spectacular horseman. With the outbreak of the Civil War he is made a lieutenant and assigned to the Michigan Brigade. By an absurd clerical error—totally unfounded in fact—he is appointed a brigadier general and leads the Michigan cavalry in spirited charges that rout the Confederate forces. A brisk montage then flashes the locations of Custer's other victories.

At war's end he is reduced to the rank of captain (factual) and, like most officers of that period, left without an assignment. Through his wife's influence, he is appointed lieutenant colonel of the newly formed Seventh Cavalry and sent to Fort Lincoln in the Dakota Territory to quell the Indians and help effect colonization.

In 1876 he accuses certain business parties of violating Indian treaties and arouses the ire of U. S. Grant, who as a soldier despises Custer and as the president considers him dangerous. Custer's accusations cause him to be suspended from his command, but his wife pleads with her friend General Philip Sheridan, commander in chief of the army (also factual), and Custer is allowed to take command of his regiment to subdue the Indian uprisings.

He leads his men to what he knows will be certain death for all of them and leaves with his wife papers that will fix the blame on crooked businessmen and politicians. The picture ends as Sheridan, at the inquiry, turns to Mrs. Custer and says, "Come, my dear—your soldier won his final victory." Would that history could be so rewritten.

As a point of departure for a study of Custer *They Died with Their Boots On* has much to offer. But its best offering is a spankingly well-made adventure yarn, with Errol Flynn at the top of his form as a storybook hero and the delightful Olivia de Havilland, in her eighth and final role with Flynn, as the best wife any soldier ever had.

46

Joan Fontaine, Billy Bevan and Cary Grant.

Suspicion

1941

An RKO-Radio Production; produced by Carroll Clark; directed by Alfred Hitchcock, screenplay by Samson Raphaelson, Joan Harrison, and Alma Reville, based on the novel *Before the Fact*, by Frances Iles; photographed by Harry Stradling; musical score by Franz Waxman; running time, 99 minutes.

Cast: Cary Grant (*Johnnie Aysgarth*), Joan Fontaine (*Lina McLaidlaw*), Sir Cedric Hardwicke (*General McLaidlaw*), Nigel Bruce (*Beaky*), Dame May Whitty (*Mrs. McLaidlaw*), Isabel Jeans (*Mrs. Newsham*), Heather Angel (*Ethel*), Auriol Lee (*Isobel Sedbusk*), Reginald Sheffield (*Reggie Wetherby*), Leo G. Carroll (*Captain Melbeck*).

In the hands of a director other than Alfred Hitchcock, *Suspicion* would probably be tedious. The story is slight, and its entire effectiveness rests on Hitchcockian devices. It also owes its credibility to Joan Fontaine's performance in a role very similar to the one she had just completed with Hitchcock in *Rebecca*, that of a shy young English girl who marries a mysterious man.

However, whereas Olivier's Maxim de Winter in *Rebecca* is an aloof fellow, tormented by bitter memories, Cary Grant's Johnnie Aysgarth in *Suspicion* is a roguish playboy, charming but unprincipled, who gives his timid wife reason to wonder just what kind of a man he is.

The film was a problem for Cary Grant. In the original story the husband was a wife murderer, but Grant's popularity had been built on his easy charm and his devilish good looks. The producers worried that it would be disastrous to present him as a killer. Instead they settled for him as a cad and a tease who would prove substantial in the end. To do this effectively Hitchcock had to create an atmosphere of doubt and fear for the wife, and he was superbly assisted in this by Joan Fontaine in her subtle performance as a woman gradually unnerved by apprehension. Bits of evidence lead her to believe that her husband is a killer and that she is an intended victim.

In reviewing the picture for *The New York Times* Bosley Crowther credited Hitchcock with building "out of slight suggestions and vague, uncertain thoughts, a mounting tower of suspicion which looms forbiddingly. And this he does magnif-

48

icently with his customary casualness. An early remark dropped by the girl's father to the effect that her intended is a cheat, a scene in which the husband acts strangely indifferent to a friend when the latter is seized with a heart attack, a little squabble over a slight untruth—all are directed by Mr. Hitchcock so that they seem inconsequential at the time but still with a sinister undertone which grows as the tension mounts."

Crowther went on to say that Joan Fontaine deserved unstinting praise for her performance. The industry agreed, and Fontaine won the 1941 Academy Award for best actress.

Cary Grant, Joan Fontaine and Nigel Bruce.

Joan Fontaine and Dame May Whitty.

Central — Cary Grant, Joan Fontaine and Sir Cedric Hardwicke.

49

Donald Crisp, Roddy McDowall and Sara Allgood.

How Green Was My Valley

1941

A 20th Century-Fox Production; produced by Darryl F. Zanuck; directed by John Ford; screenplay by Philip Dunne, based on the novel by Richard Llewellyn; photographed by Arthur Miller; musical score by Alfred Newman; running time, 118 minutes.

Cast: Walter Pidgeon (*Mr. Gruffydd*), Maureen O'Hara (*Angharad*), Donald Crisp (*Mr. Morgan*), Anna Lee (*Bronwyn*), Roddy McDowall (*Huw*), John Loder (*Ianto*), Sara Allgood (*Mrs. Morgan*), Barry Fitzgerald (*Cyfartha*), Patric Knowles (*Ivor*), Morton Lowry (*Mr. Jonas*), Arthur Shields (*Parry*), Ann Todd (*Cienwen*), Fredric Worlock (*Dr. Richards*), Richard Fraser (*Davy*), Evan S. Evans (*Gwilym*), James Monks (*Owen*), Rhys Williams (*Dai Bando*), Clifford Severn (*Mervyn*), Lionel Pape (*Mr. Evans*), Ethel Griffies (*Mrs. Nicholas*), Eve March (*Meillyn Lewis*), Marten Lamont (*Iestyn Evans*), Irving Pichel (*Narrator*).

51

One of the few criticisms leveled at John Ford was his tendency to indulge in sentiment. Moments of sentimentality marred some of his later films, and yet in *How Green Was My Valley*, the story of a family and a passing way of life, Ford skillfully avoided the obvious emotional traps. This lengthy, beautifully made film deals intimately with the lives of totally believable characters, with such conviction that no sensitive viewer can fail to become sentimental in recalling it.

As a story teller Ford had a magical touch, and he was particularly astute in his pictorial values. This film, for example, has an uncanny sense of time and place. It tells a Welsh story; yet not a second of it was filmed in Wales. Fox built Ford a Welsh village in the hills north of Los Angeles, and he peopled it with several hundred actors and extras, including all the Welsh singers he could gather to perform the choral work.

Philip Dunne made an excellent scenario of Richard Llewellyn's novel. Its focal point is the Morgan family, headed by a firm father (Donald Crisp) and a gentle but wise mother (Sara Allgood), with six sons and one lovely daughter (Maureen O'Hara). The five grown sons are, like their father, coal miners, but it is their hope that young Huw (Roddy McDowall) will grow up to something finer. The lad is sensitive and intelligent, and the story is told through him. He looks back as an older man and reflects on his valley, his family, and its people.

Huw grows up in a time of change. As a boy he sees a secure, settled way of life alter for the worse as the mine owners overwork the collieries and alienate the workers. He watches in confusion as his brothers call for unionism, a movement abhorrent to his father, and he sees them gradually drift away to live in other lands.

Befriended by a compassionate minister (Walter Pidgeon), Huw observes his sister falling in love with him and her anguish in realizing that marriage with him is impossible. Instead she marries the son of a mine owner and crosses the class barrier.

As the family fortunes decrease Huw gives up his plans to be a scholar and becomes a miner. By now the community has become shabby with the littered wastes of excessive mining, and in their greed the owners have not modernized their methods.

Mr. Morgan dies in the mines as the result of faulty equipment. As a grown man Huw leaves the valley, remembering its happy days and saying, "Men like my father cannot die. They remain a living truth in my mind."

How Green Was My Valley deservedly won a flock of Oscars and many other nominations. It was awarded an Oscar as the best picture of 1941, and John Ford received one as best director. Donald Crisp was similarly honored for his masterly performance as Mr. Morgan, and Arthur Miller received the award for his brilliant photography. The picture ran into criticism in Wales, where the California settings were clearly at variance with the actual locations of Llewellyn's story, and the Welsh also felt the film rhapsodized what some of them remembered as bitter, ugly years in their history. But for audiences other than those in Wales Ford's picture, with its beauty and its sadness and its roster of splendid actors, is nearly impossible to resist.

Sara Allgood, Evan S. Evans, Donald Crisp, John Loder, James Monks, Richard Fraser and Patric Knowles.

Walter Pidgeon and Maureen O'Hara.

Greta Garbo, Melvyn Douglas and Roland Young.

Two Faced Woman

1941

An MGM Production; produced by Gottfried Reinhardt; directed by George Cukor; screenplay by S. N. Behrman, Salka Viertel, and George Oppenheimer, suggested by a play by Ludwig Fulda; photographed by Joseph Ruttenberg; musical score by Bronislau Kaper; running time, 95 minutes.

Cast: Greta Garbo (*Karin Borg*), Melvyn Douglas (*Larry Blake*), Constance Bennett (*Griselda Vaughn*), Roland Young (*O. O. Miller*), Robert Sterling (*Dick Williams*), Ruth Gordon (*Miss Ellis*), George P. Huntley, Jr. (*Mr. Wilson*), George Cleveland (*Sheriff*), Connie Cilchrist (*Miss Dunbar*), Frances Carson (*Receptionist*), James Spencer (*Carl*), William Tannen (*Ski Guide*), John Marsden (*Graham*), Olive Blakeney (*Phyllis*).

Greta Garbo made only thirteen sound films, beginning with *Anna Christie* in 1930. The least successful of them all was the last, *Two Faced Woman*. A mere thirty-seven years old and still incredibly beautiful, Garbo decided to retire from the screen. All attempts since then—and they have been numerous—have failed to bring her back. Whether she was an actress of great ability remains a subject for debate among film buffs, but she certainly was an enchanting woman, and her apparent shyness and dislike of publicity made her even more mysteriously appealing.

In late 1941 her admirers rushed to see *Two Faced Woman*—two years having passed since her last picture, the delightful *Ninotchka*—and were aghast to find that MGM had put her in a sexy, knockabout comedy. One critic summed up the reaction by saying that it was like watching one's mother getting drunk.

The film's title alludes, not to a woman of deceit, but to one who assumes another guise for a specific reason. The story begins in a ritzy ski resort in the mountains with a playboy-publisher (Melvyn Douglas) falling in love with his ski instructor (Garbo) and marrying her. This surprises his sophisticated New York–playwright girlfriend (Constance Bennett), who decides she wants him back.

Although Douglas had promised to give up the roaming life, he accepts Bennett's offer to attend the rehearsals of her new play, making his somewhat insecure wife think she will lose him. She decides to invent a twin sister for herself, a glamorous, chic, and vibrant vamp to out-Bennett Bennett.

The plan succeeds enormously. Men, including Douglas, are drawn to the sister like bears to honey. Disappointed that her husband would make a play for his sister-in-law, Garbo retreats to her ski resort. He follows her and manages to persuade her that he knew all along that she was the same woman. But did he?

For Garbo fanatics *Two Faced Woman* was offensive; for others it was merely amusing. It caused a little commotion at the time among the censors and other arbiters of public morality, since it dealt with a woman playing her own sister and seemingly having an affair with the husband. In any event, it is still a pleasure to see the film for the sake of the divine Garbo and the polished performance of the smooth Melvyn Douglas, the kind of gentleman-actor now almost extinct.

Greta Garbo, Robert Sterling and Roland Young.

Constance Bennett, Melvyn Douglas and Greta Garbo.

Woman of the Year

Spencer Tracy, Katharine Hepburn and Reginald Owen.

1942

An MGM Production; produced by Joseph L. Mankiewicz; directed by George Stevens; screenplay by Ring Lardner, Jr., and Michael Kanin; photographed by Joseph Ruttenberg; musical score by Franz Waxman; running time, 112 minutes.

Cast: Spencer Tracy (*Sam Craig*), Katharine Hepburn (*Tess Harding*), Fay Bainter (*Ellen Whitcomb*), Reginald Owen (*Clayton*), Minor Watson (*William Harding*), William Bendix (*Pinkie Peters*), Gladys Blake (*Flo Peters*), Dan Tobin (*Gerald*), Roscoe Karns (*Phil Wittaker*), William Tannen (*Ellis*), Ludwig Stossel (*Doctor Martin Lubbeck*), Sara Haden (*Refugee Home Matron*), Edith Evanston (*Alma*), George Kezas (*Chris*), Jimmy Conlin (*Reporter*), Henry Roquemore (*Justice of the Peace*).

The teaming of Katharine Hepburn and Spencer Tracy was brought about by Miss Hepburn herself. She acquired the rights to the screenplay *Woman of the Year* and sold it to Louis B. Mayer, stipulating the deal and the terms with all the confidence born of her great success with *The Philadelphia Story*. Not only did Mayer accept, but he signed her to a long-term contract, rather than face any future business hagglings with her.

She demanded Tracy as leading man, even though she had never met him, because in her mind he was perfect for the part. It was an inspired choice. Not only was Tracy perfect for this film, but he was the perfect man for Hepburn. For the remaining twenty-five years of his life they were the closest of friends, and had Tracy not been a devout Catholic, averse to divorce, they would surely have married.

Woman of the Year is a deft battle-of-the-sexes comedy with Hepburn as an esteemed newspaper columnist of firm opinions and Tracy as a sports writer on the same payroll. Each is rather contemptuous of the other's work, but once they get to know each other these two dissimilar, independent souls fall in love and marry.

It is not an easy marriage because of the differences in their interests and particularly because the lady columnist is a disaster in the kitchen. She knows little of domesticity and she is far too busy and successful at her work to pay attention to her role as wife. When he gets drunk in disgust, she tries to help him by writing his sports column, but she does it so ludicrously that she makes him appear ridiculous. It does, however, serve to bring them back together. She comes to realize the discrepancy between her domestic performance and her being elected Woman of the Year for her career activities, and when she attends her father's remarriage, the wording of the ceremony takes on new meaning for her.

As actors Tracy and Hepburn were masterful in their timing and in balancing their byplay. This was due, of course, not only to their skill, but also to their deep personal regard for one another. The public recognized this man-woman chemistry and demanded more. In all there were nine Tracy-Hepburn films, ending with *Guess Who's Coming to Dinner* in 1967. Tracy always took top billing. That fact alone is an indication of the way he and the otherwise dominant Hepburn worked so well together.

Roscoe Karns and Spencer Tracy.

Ronald Reagan, Nancy Coleman and Robert Cummings.

Kings Row

1942

A Warner Bros. Production; produced by Hal B. Wallis; directed by Sam Wood; screenplay by Casey Robinson, based on the novel by Henry Bellaman; photographed by James Wong Howe; musical score by Erich Wolfgang Korngold; running time, 127 minutes.

Cast: Ann Sheridan (*Randy Monohan*), Robert Cummings (*Parris Mitchell*), Ronald Reagan (*Drake McHugh*), Charles Coburn (*Doctor Henry Gordon*), Betty Field (*Cassandra Tower*), Claude Rains (*Doctor Alexander Tower*), Judith Anderson (*Mrs. Gordon*), Nancy Coleman (*Louise Gordon*), Karen Verne (*Elise Sandor*), Maria Ouspenskaya (*Madame Von Eln*), Harry Davenport (*Colonel Skeffington*), Ernest Cossart (*Pa Monohan*), Pat Moriarty (*Tom Monohan*), Ilka Gruning (*Ann*), Minor Watson (*Sam Winters*), Ludwig Stossel (*Doctor Berdoff*), Erwin Kalser (*Mr. Sandor*), Egon Brecher (*Doctor Candell*), Ann Todd (*Randy as a child*), Scotty Beckett (*Parris as a child*), Douglas Croft (*Drake as a child*), Mary Thomas (*Cassandra as a child*), Joan Du Valle (*Louise as a child*).

Made at a time when the emphasis was on light-hearted films for the wartime audiences, *Kings Row* was a doubtful undertaking for Warner Bros. Even after it was completed they held back its release for almost a year. Henry Bellaman's massive novel of life in a small American town at the turn of the century was heavy on dark drama, and the film faithfully followed Bellaman's accounts of murder, madness, and sadism.

Heading the cast of such a somber and adult story with Robert Cummings, Ann Sheridan, and Ronald Reagan seemed incredible to Hollywood at the time, since these were players of light material. All doubts proved groundless. *Kings Row* was critically acclaimed and widely accepted by audiences everywhere. Cummings, Sheridan, and Reagan proved highly capable in playing difficult dramatic roles, and from such superb actors as Claude Rains, Betty Field, Charles Coburn, and Judith Anderson the film gained intriguing dimensions. *Kings Row* is, in short, a masterpiece.

The town of Kings Row boasts that it is a good place to live. First appearances seem to bear this out, but as the film progresses certain undercurrents

give lie to the claim. The protagonist is Parris Mitchell (Cummings), a young medical student in love with Cassandra (Fields), the daughter of the doctor (Rains) with whom Parris studies. The doctor keeps his mad wife confined to the house, and when he realizes that his daughter is doomed to madness he kills her and commits suicide.

Parris's good friend Drake McHugh (Reagan) is a lighthearted lad from a wealthy family who enjoys the company of many girls. Louise Gordon (Nancy Coleman) loves him, but her humorless, narrow-minded parents, Doctor and Mrs. Henry Gordon (Coburn and Anderson), refuse to let her see Drake.

Another girl who loves Drake is Randy (Sheridan), a sensible and pleasant girl from a working-class family, and it is she who stands by Drake when he is financially wiped out. He takes a job in a railroad yard, and when he is injured in an accident Doctor Gordon operates and unnecessarily amputates both legs. This action brings on an outpouring of loathing from his daughter.

Robert Cummings and Claude Rains.

Betty Field and Robert Cummings.

Ann Sheridan, Ronald Reagan and Robert Cummings.

Parris meanwhile leaves for Vienna to study medicine and psychiatry. His letters are a source of strength to the crippled Drake, now married to Randy. When Parris returns to Kings Row he finds many changes for the better but he also finds it necessary to shock Drake out of his lethargy and give him a sense of optimism. Visiting his former home, sold to newcomers since the death of his beloved grandmother and guardian (Maria Ouspenskaya), Parris discovers the new residents to be charming people with a lovely daughter (Karen Verne), clearly the girl with whom his future lies.

Kings Row is excellent in every regard. Sam Wood directed his players with a sure hand, aided by some mighty talents—scriptwriter Casey Robinson, photographer James Wong Howe, production designer William Cameron Menzies, and composer Erich Wolfgang Korngold. These men were all masters in their fields, and in this film their contributions jelled magnificently.

60

Ann Sheridan and Ronald Reagan.

Alan Ladd and Veronica Lake.

This Gun for Hire

1942

A Paramount Production; produced by Richard M. Blumenthal; directed by Frank Tuttle; screenplay by Albert Maltz and W. R. Burnett, based on the novel by Graham Greene; photographed by John Seitz; musical score by David Buttolph; running time, 80 minutes.

Cast: Veronica Lake (*Ellen Graham*), Robert Preston (*Michael Crane*), Laird Cregar (*Willard Gates*), Alan Ladd (*Raven*), Tully Marshall (*Alvin Bewster*), Mikhail Rasumny (*Sluky*), Marc Lawrence (*Tommy*), Pamela Blake (*Annie*), Harry Shannon (*Steve Finnerty*), Frank Ferguson (*Albert Baker*), Bernadene Hayes (*Baker's Secretary*), Olin Howard (*Blair Fletcher*), Roger Imhof (*Senator Burnett*), Patricia Farr (*Ruby*).

Alan Ladd had played small parts in almost twenty films by the time he was given the role of Raven in *This Gun for Hire*. He had made little impression on the public before, but as an expressionless, baby-faced killer in this film he received

immediate acclaim. From then on Ladd was a star, proving that a short man (five feet, six inches) could win admirers along with the tall ones. This was a signal victory—Hollywood stereotyping had previously set the mark for leading men at the six-foot level. But Ladd was an effective actor, and his Raven was not simply a killer, but a lonely man alienated from society, one who cannot bring himself to kill a young girl even though she is the only witness to a murder he has committed.

Paramount updated Graham Greene's *A Gun for Sale,* which they had purchased in 1936, and gave it a wartime-American setting. The plot remained much the same—a gunman is hired to kill a scientist and obtain secret documents. In this version the employers are foreign agents and the documents concern formulas for new explosives. The gunman is cheated by being paid off with marked stolen money, and he resolves to kill the principal agent (Laird Cregar) for turning him into a fugitive. At the same time the FBI enlists the aid of a nightclub singer–magician (Veronica Lake) in trapping the same agent. She accepts, with the understanding

Laird Cregar and Alan Ladd.

that her assignment will be kept secret, even from the police detective (Robert Preston) she hopes to marry. The paths of the pursued and his various pursuers crisscross through industrial sites and railroad yards and end in the offices of a munitions magnate, where both the agent and Raven die.

Ladd received fourth billing in *This Gun for Hire*, but his impact on the public was so great that Paramount quickly rushed him into star status in *The Glass Key*, continuing his guise as a quiet little tough guy. The film similarly increased the popularity of Veronica Lake. Her scenes with Ladd are particularly effective as she takes pity on the killer and stirs some emotion in him. As a diminutive beauty of five feet two she was physically a good match. She starred with Ladd in *The Glass Key*, did a take-off skit with him in *Duffy's Tavern* (1945) and starred with him in two other rough-and-tough crime pictures—*The Blue Dahlia* (1946) and *Saigon* (1948).

Alan Ladd, Laird Cregar, Victor Kilian, and Tully Marshall.

Bob Hope and Madeleine Carroll.

My Favorite Blonde

1942

A Paramount Production; produced by Paul Jones; directed by Sidney Lanfield; screenplay by Don Hartman and Frank Butler, based on a story by Norman Panama and Melvin Frank; photographed by William Mellor; musical score by David Buttolph; running time, 78 minutes.

Cast: Bob Hope (*Larry Haines*), Madeleine Carroll (*Karen Bentley*), Gale Sondergaard (*Madame Stephanie Runick*), George Zucco (*Doctor Hugo Streger*), Lionel Royce (*Karl*), Walter Kingsford (*Doctor Faber*), Victor Varconi (*Miller*), Otto Reichow (*Lanz*), Charles Cane (*Turk O'Flaherty*), Crane Whitley (*Ulrich*), Erville Anderson (*Sheriff*), Esther Howard (*Mrs. Topley*), Ed Gargan (*Mulrooney*), James Burke (*Union Secretary*), Dooley Wilson (*Porter*).

As a movie comedian of the forties, Bob Hope was a one-man industry. He appeared in twenty films, as well as making innumerable radio broadcasts and traveling countless thousands of miles to entertain the armed forces all over the world. His films in this period were consistently well written, and *My Favorite Blonde* is both typical of them all and the best of them.

Hope's characterization in all these pictures was that of a brash, quick-witted young man, usually down on his luck, rather cowardly, and a little dishonest and always on the make for money and girls. In *Blonde* he is a third-rate vaudevillian, playing second banana to a penguin. He runs into a beautiful British spy, played by Madeleine Carroll, whose cool, elegant refinement made for an improbable but amusing pairing. The film gave the ladylike

65

Walter Kingsford, Madeleine Carroll and Bob Hope.

Madeleine a rare opportunity to clown, and she performed delightfully.

In brief this cockeyed yarn concerns Madeleine's efforts to make her way across the United States in possession of plans involving the shipment of aircraft to England, all the time pursued by Nazis eager to get the plans. In New York she stumbles into Hope's dingy dressing room. His performing penguin has been hired by a Hollywood studio, requiring him to make a trip to California, where she must also proceed.

She begs for his help, and the poor idiot is powerless to resist. Together they travel in all kinds of conveyances, hounded all the way by murderous agents of the Third Reich. To elude their pursuers they use various disguises, including an involvement as an Irish bride and groom at a truckdrivers' picnic.

Much of the film's fun comes from Hope's ignorance of the real danger of his situation. Whenever his faintheartedness overcomes him the lovely lady turns on her charm and appeals to a powerful part of his nature—his concupiscence. She tells him, "There's something about you, an air of . . . *je ne sais quoi.*"

To which he smugly replies, "I always use a little aftershave." With her mission a success, she thanks him and he claims, "I'd do it all over again—even if I were in my right mind."

The passage of time and an overfamiliarity with Bob Hope's comedic style has drained *My Favorite Blonde* of some of its humor, but much of it remains. If nothing else, the film serves to remind us that the delectable Madeleine Carroll was indeed a favorite blonde and that penguins are excruciatingly funny little creatures.

Victor Mature and Rita Hayworth.

My Gal Sal

1942

A 20th Century-Fox Production; produced by Robert Bassler; directed by Irving Cummings, screenplay by Seton I. Miller, Darrell Ware, and Karl Tunberg, based on *My Brother Paul,* by Theodore Dreiser; photographed in Technicolor by Ernest Palmer; musical direction by Alfred Newman; running time, 103 minutes.

Cast: Rita Hayworth (*Sally Elliott*), Victor Mature (*Paul Dresser*), John Sutton (*Fred Haviland*), Carole Landis (*Mae Collins*), James Gleason (*Pat Hawley*), Phil Silvers (*Wiley*), Walter Catlett (*Colonel Truckee*), Mona Maris (*Countess Rossini*), Frank Orth (*McGuinness*), Stanley Andrews (*Mr. Dreiser*), Margaret Moffat (*Mrs. Dreiser*), Libby Taylor (*Ida*), John Kelly (*John L. Sullivan*), Curt Bois (*De Rochemont*), Gregory Gaye (*Garnier*), Andrew Tombes (*Henri*).

The distinguished American novelist Theodore Dreiser had a brother who was not nearly so distinguished but was a much more colorful character.

Paul, born in Terre Haute, Indiana, in 1860, joined a traveling theatrical troupe when he was twenty and anglicized his name to Dresser. He was a songwriter and a promoter on Broadway for a few glittering years before dying at the age of forty-six in 1905.

When he wrote *My Brother Paul,* Theodore Dreiser pulled no punches in painting his older brother as a bit of a rogue, and when they made the film about him, Fox made a good choice with Victor Mature as Dresser. Brashness was Mature's forte, and in *My Gal Sal* he swaggered in a winning manner.

Lest the public fear that this was merely an account of a pushy songwriter, the studio gave top billing to Rita Hayworth as the love of Dresser's life, Sally Elliott, a glamorous musical star of the period.

Oddly for a movie about a composer, Fox decided to bolster the selection of Dresser songs with a half dozen new ones, albeit in period style, by Leo Robin and Ralph Rainger. Of the Dresser songs only the title ballad and "On the Banks of the

John Sutton, Rita Hayworth, Victor Mature, Mona Maris and James Gleason.

Rita Hayworth and Phil Silvers.

Wabash" are well-known, and none of the new songs became popular, although the memory of Hayworth singing "Oh, the Pity of It All" is pleasant. Hayworth won praise for her singing, and Fox concealed the fact that it was dubbed by Nan Wynn.

My Gal Sal is an excellent presentation of musical life on Broadway in the 1890s. Director Irving Cummings (1888–1959) spent his early career in New York, and his knowledge of and interest in the period are clear in many touches throughout the picture.

The film follows Dresser from his road-show days and even shows him being tarred and feathered and run out of a town as part of fake medicine act. Ambition drives him on and on, and in New York he falls madly in love with a top musical-comedy star. She likes his material and performs it in the theater, bringing him the fame he seeks.

Winning *her* proves to be much harder, since he seems to her to be intent mainly on getting ahead in show business. But Dresser never gives up, and when he writes a song just for her, "My Gal Sal," she gives in.

This genial and entertaining movie avoids pointing out that this was actually the last song Paul Dresser wrote and that he died a year later.

Now, Voyager

1942

A Warner Bros. Production; produced by Hal B. Wallis; directed by Irving Rapper; screenplay by Casey Robinson, based on the novel by Olive Higgins Prouty; photographed by Sol Polito; musical score by Max Steiner; running time, 118 minutes.

Cast: Bette Davis (*Charlotte Vale*), Paul Henreid (*Jerry Durence*), Claude Rains (*Doctor Jaquith*), Gladys Cooper (*Mrs. Vale*), Bonita Granville (*June Vale*), John Loder (*Elliott Livingston*), Ilka Chase (*Lisa Vale*), Lee Patrick (*Deb McIntyre*), James Rennie (*Frank McIntyre*), Charles Drake (*Leslie Trotter*), Katharine Alexander (*Miss Trask*), Janis Wilson (*Tina*), Mary Wickes (*Donna Pickford*), Michael Ames (*Doctor Regan*), Franklin Pangborn (*Mr. Thompson*).

Bette Davis was the queen of Hollywood actresses during the forties. In seventeen major features she won both respect and popularity as a woman of great talent and strong personality. All through the thirties she had fought her employers for better material, and by 1940 there was no doubt about either her skill or her courage.

The quintessential Davis film of the forties is *Now, Voyager.* It can well be argued that *The Letter* (1940) and *The Little Foxes* (1941) were better films, but in terms of public acceptance and identification *Now, Voyager* heads the list. It is, of course, soap opera and as such the best of its kind, shining with Warner Bros. expertise and backed with a lush Max Steiner musical score that is almost as much a part of the picture as the actors. The main musical theme quickly took on a life of its own—with lyrics put to it by Kim Gannon, it became the song "It Can't Be Wrong" and forever part of the sound of 1942.

This was also the film in which Paul Henreid lit two cigarettes simultaneously, then gallantly gave one to Miss Davis, thereby starting a new custom.

What makes *Now, Voyager* especially memorable is the poignancy of Miss Davis's performance as Charlotte Vale, a repressed ugly duckling blossoming into an attractive and kindly woman. Charlotte is spiritually downtrodden by her mother (Gladys

Paul Henreid and Bette Davis.

Cooper) in their wealthy Boston home. Her sister-in-law (Ilka Chase) brings in a psychiatrist (Claude Rains), a worldly-wise gentleman who persuades Charlotte to rest in a sanitarium and to undergo analysis.

Within a few months there are noticeable changes in the young woman—she becomes more assured and more interested in life. She takes a boat trip to South America and meets a suave gentleman, Jerry Durrence (Henreid), with whom she falls in love. He explains that despite his feelings for her he cannot return her love because he is married.

Later in Boston Charlotte passes up an opportunity for a marriage into high society. Her mother becomes so angry over this that she suffers a fatal heart attack. Beset by guilt, Charlotte retreats to the sanitarium, but she is saved from her own depression when she befriends a young girl, Tina Durrence (Janis Wilson), the daughter of Jerry and unwanted by her own ailing mother.

Jerry visits them, and although the unrequited-love situation remains the same, Charlotte realizes that she at least has the love and companionship of his daughter.

In less capable hands *Now, Voyager* would have been sentimental nonsense, but Bette Davis makes its heroine a touching, dignified, and truly believable woman.

Bette   Davis,   Claude
Rains   and   Ilka   Chase.

Bette Davis and Gladys Cooper.

Bing Crosby, Dorothy Lamour and Bob Hope.

Road to Morocco

1942

A Paramount Production; produced by Paul Jones; directed by David Butler; screenplay by Frank Butler and Don Hartman; photographed by William C. Mellor; songs by Johnny Burke and Jimmy Van Heusen; musical direction by Victor Young; running time, 83 minutes.

Cast: Bing Crosby (*Jeff Peters*), Bob Hope (*Turkey Jackson*), Dorothy Lamour (*Princess Shalmar*), Anthony Quinn (*Mullay Kasim*), Donna Drake (*Mihirmah*), Mikhail Rasumny (*Ahmed Fey*), Vladimir Sokoloff (*Hyder Khan*), George Givot (*Neb Jolla*), Andrew Tombes (*Oso Bucco*), Leon Belasco (*Yusef*).

Paramount's lucrative *Road* series, with Bing Crosby, Bob Hope, and Dorothy Lamour, evolved

Anthony Quinn, and the heads of Crosby and Hope.

Bing Crosby, Dorothy Lamour and Vladimir Sokoloff.

in a casual way. The studio had bought a story titled *The Road to Mandalay,* a dramatic adventure yarn, and then had doubts about filming it. They decided to turn it into a comedy for George Burns and Gracie Allen, but the couple didn't like it. The studio next showed it to Fred MacMurray and Jack Oakie. They didn't care for it either, but Crosby and Hope, who had been friends for some time and were looking for a vehicle they could do together, agreed to tackle this script provided they could kick it around and ab lib. Retitled *The Road to Singapore* and released in 1940, it caught the public fancy and clearly cried for a sequel.

The studio dusted off another dead script, and writers Frank Butler and Don Hartman performed the same comic revitalizing they had done with the previous one, the result being *The Road to Zanzibar* (1941). But for the next one Paramount told them to concoct their own material—and a good argument can be made that *The Road to Morocco* is the best of the whole line.

In this one the two are shipwrecked and washed up on the shores of Morocco, where Crosby, always the opportunist, sells Hope, always the dupe, into slavery to make a little money and to get into the palace and establish useful contacts.

Crosby casts a covetous eye on the lovely Princess Shalmar (Lamour), but she is betrothed to a virile and jealous sheik (Anthony Quinn).

Hope is delighted to find himself pampered and coddled by a bevy of harem beauties—until he discovers that it's all part of his preparation for sacrificial death. With the help of the princess, who has fallen in love with him, Crosby comes to his aid, and in company with a pretty little harem girl (Donna Drake), who has taken a shine to Hope, they all escape.

At film's end they are on a raft in the ocean, and Hope goes into a dramatic frenzy about thirst, starvation, and death. Crosby interrupts, and Hope complains that Crosby has ruined Hope's best scene in the picture and a chance to win an Oscar.

The Road to Morocco is a torrent of visual and verbal gags, many of them directed straight at the audience. For example, a camel says, "This is the screwiest picture I've ever been in." The whole happy enterprise is also aided by a good selection of songs by Burke and Van Heusen, especially the witty title number and the beguiling "Moonlight Becomes You." Hope and Crosby subsequently took roads to Utopia (1946), Rio (1948), Bali (1953), and Hong Kong (1962).

Joel McCrea and Claudette Colbert.

The Palm Beach Story

1942

A Paramount Production; produced by Paul Jones; directed and written by Preston Sturges; photographed by Victor Milner; musical score by Victor Young; running time, 88 minutes.

Cast: Claudette Colbert (*Gerry Jeffers*); Joel McCrea (*Tom Jeffers*); Mary Astor (*Princess*); Rudy Vallee (*John D. Hackensacker III*); Franklin Pangborn (*Apartment Manager*); Robert Dudley (*The Wienie King*); Sig Arno (*Toto*); William Demarest, Robert Warwick, Arthur Stuart Hill, Torben Meyer, Jimmy Conlin, Vic Potel, Jack Norton, Robert Greig, Roscoe Ates, Dewey Robinson, Chester Conklin, Sheldon Jett (*Members of the Ale and Quail Club*).

Preston Sturges followed *The Lady Eve* with *Sullivan's Travels*, in which he spoofed Hollywood, and then turned his devastatingly probing wit on the affairs of the American idle rich. *The Palm Beach Story* actually takes its momentum from the predicament of not having money. A handsome young married couple, Tom and Gerry Jeffers (Joel McCrea and Claudette Colbert), are still deeply in love after five years of marriage, but they are desperate for lack of cash. He is an inventor unable to interest backers in his revolutionary ideas. His wife decides that the only way she can help him is to divorce him, land a wealthy new husband, and then subsidize Tom.

As they are about to give up their apartment, a strange little half-deaf old man wanders in to take a look at it and announces that he is America's Wienie King (Robert Dudley). This elfin character is so unconcerned about his wealth that he carries wads of bills in his pockets, and when he hears of Gerry's troubles he simply shoves money into her

77

Rudy Vallee and Claudette Colbert.

hands. With this she takes a train to Palm Beach, Florida.

The train ride turns out to be quite an experience. Gerry is swept along by the boisterous generosity of the Ale and Quail Club, a band of millionaires off on a hunting spree. These wealthy buffoons think nothing of firing their shotguns inside the train, and in order to be rid of them the conductors unhitch the club car and leave it on a siding. Gerry, still in the club car and out of cash, cunningly brings herself to the attention of mild-mannered John D. Hackensacker III (Rudy Vallee) and easily wangles herself into his affections. She accepts his invitation to cruise with him on his yacht and to be his house guest.

Gerry now comes into contact with his man-hungry sister (Mary Astor), whom he calls Princess because she was once married to a prince. The irate

Tom also arrives on the scene, furious that his wife has left him and firmly intent on taking her home. But Gerry persuades him to pose as her brother, because she thinks she can get from Hackensacker the capital to back Tom's plans for a downtown airport.

Hackensacker proposes marriage, and Princess decides that the handsome Tom is next on her list. The morass of complications subsides when Gerry and Tom reveal that they both have identical twins, and the film ends with a double wedding.

Sturges enjoyed needling the superwealthy for their arrogance and their dizzy social life, but in *The Palm Beach Story* he did it without being malicious. He was a satirist with a fondness for humankind, and even the absurd Hackensacker and Princess, finely played by Vallee and Astor, come off as warmly understandable people.

Joel McCrea, Claudette Colbert and Rudy Vallee.

Joel McCrea, Rudy Vallee, Mary Astor and Claudette Colbert.

Joel McCrea (twice), Claudette Colbert (twice), with Rudy Vallee, Mary Astor and Sig Arno.

Charles Bates, Henry Travers, Edna May Wonacott, Teresa Wright and Joseph Cotten.

Shadow of a Doubt

1943

A Universal Production; produced by Jack H. Skirball; directed by Alfred Hitchcock; screenplay by Thornton Wilder, Sally Benson, and Alma Reville, based on a story by Gordon McDonell; photographed by Joseph Valentine; musical score by Dimitri Tiomkin; running time, 108 minutes.

Cast: Teresa Wright (*Young Charlie*), Joseph Cotten (*Uncle Charlie*), Macdonald Carey (*Jack Graham*), Patricia Collinge (*Emma Newton*), Henry Travers (*Joseph Newton*), Hume Cronyn (*Herbie Hawkins*), Wallace Ford (*Fred Saunders*), Edna May Wonacott (*Ann Newton*), Charles Bates (*Roger Newton*), Irving Bacon (*Station Master*), Clarence Muse (*Pullman Porter*), Janet Shaw (*Louise*), Estelle Jewell (*Catharine*).

Alfred Hitchcock cites *Shadow of a Doubt* as a favorite among his own films. It is a perfect example of this wily director's particular style as a film-

maker, the core of which is setting up macabre vibrations in seemingly calm and commonplace surroundings. In this case Hitchcock insisted on filming his story in an actual small town—a revolutionary consideration for Hollywood in 1943. He chose Santa Rosa, California, and he picked Thornton Wilder as one of his scenarists, to give the picture as much folksy Americana as possible.

The doubts that begin to shadow the story are caused by a genial gentleman's visit to his relatives in Santa Rosa. Uncle Charlie (Joseph Cotten) descends from across the country to stay with his sister and her family, to the delight of his pretty niece and namesake, Young Charlie (Teresa Wright). Uncle and niece have a feeling of rapport, mostly because she has heard about him all her life but never met him. After a while, however, she begins to sense that there is something strange about him, something that he is keeping to himself.

Their spiritual closeness is not shared by the other relatives. They see Uncle Charlie as a moody

80

but ordinary fellow, while Young Charlie grows to suspect him of terrible doings. It turns out that he is a murderer, having disposed of three wives to gain their money. The niece fears that revealing this knowledge will cause her own death, but circumstances bring about Uncle Charlie's demise before this can happen. Charlie's relatives bury him as a respectable citizen, and only the niece knows otherwise.

Hitchcock's devilish cat-and-mouse techniques give *Shadow of a Doubt* an arresting sense of suspense, and his decision to tell his tale in this attractive little town was inspired. So too was his choice of Joseph Cotten and Teresa Wright as his leads. Cotten is superb as the mysterious uncle, whose charm diminishes in the eyes of his niece as his potential for harm increases, and Miss Wright, always a subtle and affecting actress, is uncomfortably believable in delineating the niece's predicament. Their acting—plus the many Hitchcockian touches—makes this a spellbinding picture.

Patricia Collinge, Teresa Wright, Joseph Cotten, Macdonald Carey and Wallace Ford.

Joseph Cotten and Teresa Wright.

Teresa Wright and Macdonald Carey.

Ida Lupino and Joan
Leslie.

The Hard Way

Ida Lupino, Joan Leslie and Roman Bohnen.

1943

A Warner Bros. Production; produced by Jerry
Wald; directed by Vincent Sherman; screenplay by
Daniel Fuchs and Peter Viertel; photographed by
James Wong Howe; musical score by Heinz Roem-
held; running time, 97 minutes.

Cast: Ida Lupino (*Helen Chernen*), Dennis Morgan
(*Paul Collins*), Joan Leslie (*Katherine Chernen*),
Jack Carson (*Albert Runkel*), Gladys George (*Lily
Emery*), Faye Emerson (*Blonde Waitress*), Paul
Cavanagh (*John Shagrue*), Leona Maricle (*Laura
Bithorn*), Roman Bohnen (*Sam Chernen*), Ray
Montgomery (*Johnny Gilpin*), Julie Bishop (*Chor-
ine*), Nester Paiva (*Max Wade*), Joan Woodbury
(*Maria*), Ann Doran (*Dorschka*), Thurston Hall
(*Film Executive*), Lou Lubin (*Frenchy*), Jody Gil-
bert (*Anderson*).

Always a fine actress, and later in her career a
capable director, Ida Lupino never quite won the
popularity she deserved. Born in London in 1918 of

a famous theatrical family, she came to Hollywood in 1934 and straightaway started work in films. One of the most clever of her performances is in the almost forgotten *The Hard Way*, a brilliant but bitter drama directed by Vincent Sherman, who, like Miss Lupino, has not yet received sufficient credit for his craftsmanship over a long career.

The Hard Way, set in a grimy little industrial town called Greenhill, tells of the machinations of a thwarted woman, Helen Churnen (Lupino), who transfers her own career ambitions to her pretty young sister Katherine (Joan Leslie). Helen loathes her own drab life, and she is determined that Katherine will not fall into the same trap of a loveless marriage to a dumb ox of a laborer (Roman Bohnen) and a near-poverty existence.

Katherine has a little talent as a singer and dancer, and Helen pushes her into a career in show business. She spots an opportunity when a pair of song-and-dance men, Paul Collins (Dennis Morgan) and Albert Runkel (Jack Carson), play a theater in Greenhill. Runkel takes a liking to Katherine, and Helen promotes it into marriage. Collins

soon finds himself asked to leave the act and make way for the young Mrs. Runkel.

Time passes, and when Helen senses that her sister is good enough to make out as a single, she moves to break up the marriage. Katherine receives offers that take her on her way, and the deserted husband commits suicide.

Katherine finally makes it to Broadway stardom, but when Helen again tries to interfere with her love life the now confident little sister turns on Helen and totally rejects her. Helen's years of scheming finally bring her nothing.

Sherman's direction of this searing story is sure handed and uncompromising, and the photography of the brilliant James Wong Howe is sharp and dramatic. It is, however, an actor's picture. Ida Lupino is thoroughly convincing as the vicious driven woman. As the loser-husband, a pitiful figure hiding behind a bluff personality, Jack Carson gave a performance that marked him an actor of real substance. He and Dennis Morgan made a number of mildly amusing comedies together, but their best work was done in this fine film.

Jack Carson, Joan Leslie and Dennis Morgan.

Ida Lupino, Jack Carson and Dennis Morgan.

Ida Lupino, Dennis Morgan and Joan Leslie.

Dana Andrews and Henry Fonda.

The Ox-Bow Incident

1943

A 20th Century-Fox Production; produced by Lamar Trotti; directed by William Wellman; screenplay by Lamar Trotti, based on the novel by Walter Van Tilburg Clark; photographed by Arthur Miller; musical score by Cyril Mockridge; running time, 75 minutes.

Cast: Henry Fonda (*Gil Carter*), Dana Andrews (*Martin*), Mary Beth Hughes (*Rose Mapen*), Anthony Quinn (*Mexican*), William Eythe (*Gerald*), Henry Morgan (*Art Croft*), Jane Darwell (*Ma Grier*), Matt Briggs (*Judge Tyler*), Harry Davenport (*Davies*), Frank Conroy (*Major Tetley*), Marc Lawrence (*Farnley*), Victor Kilian (*Darby*), Paul Hurst (*Monty Smith*), Chris-Pin Martin (*Poncho*), Ted North (*Joyce*), George Meeker (*Mr. Swanson*), Almira Sessions (*Mrs. Swanson*), Margaret Hamilton (*Mrs. Larch*), Dick Rich (*Mapes*), Francis Ford (*Old Man*).

Henry Fonda and director William Wellman forced *The Ox-Bow Incident* on 20th Century-Fox and received a go-ahead only when they both

agreed to make certain other Fox pictures. The studio's reluctance was understandable. This off-beat, downbeat Western had few conventional entertainment values and did poorly at the box office when released. It took time for the film to be recognized as a work of cinematic art and moral integrity. *The Ox-Bow Incident* is a somber, disturbing story, a Greek tragedy in a Western setting, and it makes uncompromising comments on American lawlessness.

Two ordinary roughneck cowboys, Gil (Fonda) and Art (Henry Morgan), ride into the town of Bridger's Wells, Nevada, and head for the saloon to relax. Not long after their arrival news hits the town that a local rancher has been murdered and his cattle stolen. With the sheriff away the angry townspeople decide to take the law into their own hands. A few citizens speak out against the decision, but most of the crowd is excited by a desire for revenge and action.

Gil and Art begrudgingly answer the call for able-bodied men to form the posse. Heading them is a pompous ex Confederate officer, Major Tetley (Frank Conroy), who obviously enjoys getting back

into uniform. The mood of the posse becomes vicious, and when they discover three men around a campfire at night, they assume these men are the culprits. Bits of circumstantial evidence point to their possible guilt, and the posse swiftly decides to hang the three, a young cowboy (Dana Andrews), a stoic, defiant Mexican (Anthony Quinn), and a senile old man (Francis Ford).

The cowboy asks to write a letter to his wife and

The three victims — Anthony Quinn, Dana Andrews and Francis Ford.

Ted North, Victor Kilian, Henry Fonda, Henry Morgan and Harry Davenport.

weeps as he does so, and Gil promises to deliver the letter. The men are hanged, and the posse returns to town in a mood of satisfaction.

When the sheriff returns he tells them there has been no murder and no rustling. In the saloon Gil reads aloud the letter from the cowboy to his wife, to a sullen audience of the lynch-mob members; then he and Art quietly ride out of town to deliver the letter to the widow.

The Ox-Bow Incident has an emotional wallop that does not diminish with time. The film is somewhat marred by the obvious use of studio backdrops in the outdoor sequences, but the acting more than compensates for it. The film is a searing indictment of mob violence and an honest depiction of the crude values of frontier life, leavened here and there with figures of decency and compassion.

Joyce Renolds, Richard Ryan, Charles Boyer, Joan Fontaine and Jean Muir.

The Constant Nymph

1943

A Warner Bros. Production; produced by Henry Blanke; directed by Edmund Goulding; screenplay by Kathryn Scola, based on the novel and play by Margaret Kennedy and Basil Dean; photographed by Tony Gaudio; musical score by Erich Wolfgang Korngold; running time, 112 minutes.

Cast: Charles Boyer (*Lewis Dodd*), Joan Fontaine (*Tessa*), Alexis Smith (*Florence Creighton*), Brenda Marshall (*Toni Sanger*), Charles Coburn (*Charles Creighton*), Dame May Whitty (*Lady Longborough*), Peter Lorre (*Fritz Bercovy*), Joyce Reynolds (*Paula Sanger*), Jean Muir (*Kate Sanger*), Montagu Love (*Albert Sanger*), Eduardo Ciannelli (*Roberto*), Jeannie Crispin (*Marie*), Doris Lloyd (*Miss Hamilton*), Joan Blair (*Lina Kamaroff*), Andre Charlot (*Dr. Renee*), Richard Ryan (*Kiril Trigorin*), Crauford Kent (*Thorpe*), Marcel Dalio (*Georges*), Clemence Groves (*Concert Pianist*).

Charles Boyer, Alexis Smith, Joan Fontaine and Peter Lorre.

Charles Boyer, Joyce Reynolds and Joan Fontaine.

Margaret Kennedy's 1924 novel *The Constant Nymph* was a bestseller before being adapted into a stage play, and British companies filmed it in 1927 and 1933. This high-class melodrama concerns the life-style and the loves of concert musicians and derives much of its poignancy from delving into the artistic "soul"—the gulf between sensitive, creative artists and conventional human beings.

Warners gave full rein to producer Henry Blanke for this handsome version, and in Edmund Goulding they chose a director with some musical education. They also assigned the prestigious Erich Wolfgang Korngold to compose a landmark of a musical score that lifts this picture like a giant unseen hand. The leading character is a modern composer, played by Charles Boyer, and what he composes is actually Korngold's work. Whenever he sits at the piano to play, it is Korngold, himself a brilliant pianist, the audience hears on the sound track.

Lewis Dodd (Boyer) is a frustrated composer, hired as a tutor by a family of British musicians who live a happy Bohemian life in an Alpine home in Switzerland. When the father dies, the four now parentless daughters find their future being decided by an influential uncle (Charles Coburn) and his socially prominent daughter Florence (Alexis Smith). One of the girls, Tessa (Joan Fontaine), is deeply in love with Dodd, and she is distressed when he shows an interest in Forence. This interest leads to marriage, with both partners believing their union will lead to career fulfillment for the ambitious composer.

This proves not to be the case. Dodd feels stifled by the society in which he now lives, and his music fails to impress anyone. Tessa, unhappy at an English boarding school, understands his frustration and his need for a kindred spirit. She leaves the school, and together they write a composition, during the course of which Dodd realizes that he loves this young and ailing girl. She dies of a heart attack while listening to the premiere broadcast of the work.

Edmund Goulding skillfully worked this emotionally tenuous tale into an intelligent and touching film, with excellent performances from Boyer as the troubled composer and Joan Fontaine as the exquisite Tessa. Vying for stardom is the music score, and Korngold later published its main piece (the Dodd-Tessa work) as "Tomorrow," a tone poem for contralto, women's choir, and orchestra, his Opus 33. Author Margaret Kennedy supplied the lyrics.

Laird Cregar and Monty Woolley.

Holy Matrimony

1943

A 20th Century-Fox Production; produced by Nunnally Johnson; directed by John Stahl; screenplay by Nunnally Johnson, based on the novel *Buried Alive,* by Arnold Bennett; photographed by Lucien Ballard; musical score by Cyril Mockridge; running time, 87 minutes.

Cast: Monty Woolley (*Priam Farli*), Gracie Fields (*Alice Challice*), Laird Cregar (*Clive Oxford*)**,** Una O'Connor (*Mrs. Leek*), Alan Mowbray (*Mr. Pennington*), Melville Cooper (*Doctor Caswell*), Franklin Pangborn (*Duncan Farli*), Ethel Griffies (*Lady Vale),* Eric Blore (*Henry Leek*), Montagu Love (*Judge*), Richard Fraser (*John Leek*), Edwin Maxwell (*King Edward VII*), Ian Wolfe (*Strawley*), Alec Craig (*Aylmer*).

Monty Woolley (1888–1963), with his haughty manner, superb diction, and neatly trimmed beard, was a professor at Yale University who dabbled in dramatics and did not make his professional debut until 1936. He won fame playing *The Man Who*

Came to Dinner, the play by George S. Kaufman and Moss Hart about an imperious, cantankerous writer-pundit named Sheridan Whiteside. The part was based on Alexander Woollcott, and Monty Woolley was an entertaining personification of everything the acidly witty Woollcott could ever have been.

When Warners filmed the play in 1941 there was only one choice for the lead. Woolley's success in the film offered only one problem—finding suitable material for this very special figure. He played to advantage in *The Pied Piper* and *The Light of Heart,* and then came *Holy Matrimony,* a perfect vehicle for an actor whom nature had already typecast as a crusty highbrow.

Nunnally Johnson tailored Arnold Bennett's novel *Buried Alive* to fit Woolley, and as both writer and producer, Johnson saw to it that the picture was made precisely as he wanted it. The picture begins somewhere in the tropics, where Priam Farli (Woolley) has spent more than twenty blissful years of solitude indulging his passion for painting. His idyll is shattered by a command from

Buckingham Palace to appear in London and receive a knighthood. Arriving in England Farli, loath to give up his reclusiveness and cursing his fame, begrudgingly prepares himself. But at this point his valet suddenly dies, and the doctor mistakenly enters Farli's name on the death certificate.

The body is buried in Westminster Abbey, and through the resultant publicity a woman, Alice Challice (Gracie Fields), turns up and lays claim to a proposal of marriage she has received by mail from the valet. Rather than reveal himself, Farli marries the woman and discovers her to be an agreeable wife. He also discovers that the valet already had a wife, and this one shows up with three grown sons to whisk Farli off to court. Subsequent legal ramifications and a grueling trial clear Farli, and he settles down to married bliss and success with his paintings.

The humor of *Holy Matrimony* stems not only from the grand performance of Monty Woolley, but also from the offbeat casting of Gracie Fields as the warmhearted wife. Fields, who had appeared only in British movie musicals, here proved herself an actress of genuine ability. The public liked her teaming with Woolley so much that the two were reunited two years later in *Molly and Me*, a civilized comedy almost as good as *Holy Matrimony*.

Gracie Fields and Monty Woolley.

Monty Woolley, Gracie Fields and Laird Cregar.

Gracie Fields and Monty Woolley.

The Phantom of the Opera

1943

A Universal Production; produced by George Waggner; directed by Arthur Lubin; screenplay by Eric Taylor and Samuel Hoffenstein, adapted from the composition of Gaston Leroux by John Jacoby; photographed in Technicolor by Hal Mohr and W. Howard Greene; musical score by Edward Ward; running time, 92 minutes.

Cast: Nelson Eddy (*Anatole Carron*), Susanna Foster (*Christine Dubois*), Claude Rains (*Enrique Claudin*), Edgar Barrier (*Raoul de Chagny*), Jane Farrar (*Biancarolli*), Barbara Everest (*the Aunt*), Steve Geray (*Vercheres*), Frank Puglia (*Villeneuve*), Miles Mander (*M. Pleyel*), Hans Herbert (*Marcel*), Fritz Feld (*Lacours*), J. Edward Bromberg (*Amoit*), Hume Cronyn (*Gerard*), Gladys Blake (*Jennie*), Fritz Leiber (*Franz Liszt*).

The celebrated Lon Chaney version of *The Phantom of the Opera*, made in 1925, is a macabre and frightening film. Chaney had a genius for hideous makeup and a rare ability to communicate human anguish and despair, and any other version of this story suffers by comparison. Universal's 1943 production has a few scary moments, but it is not really a horror picture, and Claude Rains gave a more sympathetic interpretation of the title role than had Chaney.

Despite the skill of his performance, Rains had to take third billing to Nelson Eddy and Susanna Foster. With these singers as its stars, and with most of the action taking place in an opera house, great emphasis was placed on music.

This was a rich assignment for Edward Ward, who not only scored the picture but arranged the operatic sequences and provided a mini-piano concerto as the work composed by the phantom. Ward chose a scene from the third act of Von Flotow's *Martha* to open the picture and then concocted sequences using themes by Chopin and Tchaikovsky, all lustily sung by Eddy, here in excellent voice.

The phantom is actually a disfigured, embittered composer who lives in the vast sewers beneath the Paris Opera House. He becomes disfigured when he kills a music publisher who has stolen his composi-

93

Nelson Eddy and Susannah Foster.

tions and the publisher's assistant throws a pan of sulphuric acid in his face. The angonized composer retreats from society. In this screenplay he devotes himself to helping the career of a young understudy (Foster), apparently his daughter, by killing off the singers for whom the girl understudies.

A police inspector assigned to the case (Edgar Barrier) falls in love with the girl, to the chagrin of the house star (Eddy). While these two compete for the girl's affections, the phantom, now quite demented, whisks her away to the sewers and forces her to sing his music as he sits at a grand piano.

Her curiosity overcomes her, and she snatches the mask from his face, then recoils at the sight of his fearful injury.

With anger for the outside world and tenderness for the girl, the phantom is determined to keep her in his catacombs, but her suitors put an end to that scheme and the phantom goes to his death in the sewers. Of course, the opera star wins the girl, and she wins stardom.

Handsome sets, Rains's performance, Eddy's and Foster's singing, and the score by Ward make this version of *The Phantom of the Opera* a very entertaining film.

Claude Rains and Susannah Foster.

Don Ameche and Gene Tierney.

Don Ameche, Florence Bates and Laird Cregar.

Heaven Can Wait

Don Ameche, Allyn Joslyn and Gene Tierney.

96

Charles Coburn, Gene Tierney and Don Ameche.

1943

A 20th Century-Fox Production; produced and directed by Ernst Lubitsch; screenplay by Samuel Raphaelson, based on the play *Birthdays,* by Laszlo Bus-Fekete; photographed in Technicolor by Edward Cronjager; musical score by Alfred Newman; running time, 112 minutes.

Cast: Gene Tierney (*Martha*), Don Ameche (*Henry Van Cleve*), Charles Coburn (*Hugo Van Cleve*), Marjorie Main (*Mrs. Strabel*), Laird Cregar (*His Excellency*), Spring Byington (*Bertha Van Cleve*), Allyn Joslyn (*Albert Van Cleve*), Eugene Pallette (*E. F. Strabel*), Signe Hasso (*Mademoiselle*), Louis Calhern (*Randolph Van Cleve*).

Ernst Lubitsch (1892–1947) was a puckish German director who had begun his career as a comic actor. He settled in Hollywood in 1922 and gained a reputation as a filmmaker with a saucy, titillating, but never vulgar way of handling sexy comedies. He scored a great hit with *Ninotchka* in 1939, turning Garbo into an alluring comedienne, and he deftly poked fun at the German invasion of Poland in *To Be or Not to Be* (1942). The following year he used color for the first time and did it so beautifully that D. W. Griffith made a point of expressing his approval.

Heaven Can Wait is a genial film, adapted and Americanized by Samuel Ralphaelson from a Hungarian comedy. The story is set mostly in Kansas and New York in the late nineteenth century and covers the life story of Henry Van Cleve (Don Ameche), a good middle-class citizen but a bit of a Casanova.

As the film unfolds Henry arrives in hell for an appointment with the very suave, gentlemanly Satan (Laird Cregar). In a plush version of Hades, Henry relates his life story, imagining that accounting his youthful follies with various ladies will qualify him for inclusion in this realm. The sympathetic Satan thinks overwise. Henry is a better man than he believes, and his story is actually a tribute to the virtues of family life. In telling about his amorous adventures, his marriage, his children, and sundry domestic events Henry wins the respect of Satan, who turns him away and points him toward heaven.

Heaven Can Wait is a charming picture, full of warmly human Lubitsch touches, and it is a triumph in the art of set designing, its period artifacts being both accurate and tasteful. Gene Tierney played the wife with a deftness that convinced Otto Preminger that she was right for *Laura* (1944), and Don Ameche was never better than in his portrayal of Henry Van Cleve. Ameche was under contract to Fox from 1936 to 1944, and although he scored a hit playing Alexander Graham Bell in 1939, the studio generally wasted his ability on musicals and light comedies. He quit Hollywood in 1949, and in looking back over his forty films, Ameche feels that the best one is the one he most enjoyed making, *Heaven Can Wait.*

Corvette K-225

1943

A Universal Production; produced by Howard Hawks; directed by Richard Rossen; screenplay by John Rhodes Sturdy; photographed by Tony Gaudio; musical score by David Buttolph; running time, 99 minutes.

Cast: Randolph Scott (*Lieutenant Commander MacClain*), James Brown (*Sublieutenant Cartwright*), Ella Raines (*Joyce Cartwright*), Noah Beery, Jr. (*Stone*), Barry Fitzgerald (*Stokey O'Mera*), John Frederick (*First Officer*), Holmes Herbert (*Convoy Commander*), Andy Devine (*Walsh*), Fuzzy Knight (*Crickett*), Thomas Gomez (*Smithy*), David Bruce (*Lieutenant Rawlins*), Richard Lane (*Admiral*), Walter Sande (*Evans*), Oscar O'Shea (*Merchant Ship Captain*), James Flavin (*Gardner*), Murray Alper (*Jones*), Robert Mitchum (*Shephard*).

Most films Hollywood made about the Second World War, during the war, appear ridiculous now, peopled with characters so obviously heroic or villainous, depending on whether they are "our side" or "the other side." Among the handful of war movies that still deserve respect and elicit interest for their craftsmanship and their realistic look at warfare is *Corvette K-225*, which was also one of the few features to recognize Canada's involvement in the war.

The film owed its life to director Richard Rossen, who, along with photographer Tony Gaudio and a small team of assistants, spent three months on the Atlantic getting background footage and learning the facts of convoy life. They received the cooperation of the Royal Canadian Navy, which assigned Lieutenant John Rhodes Sturdy as technical advisor, and Rossen retained Sturdy to write the screenplay.

Corvettes were the backbone of convoy duty on the Atlantic, and operating them was the Canadian navy's principal contribution to the war effort. Corvettes were compact antisubmarine vessels, two hundred feet long, packed with depth charges. These rakish warships shepherded the slower-moving ships in convoy and protected them from attacks by U-boats.

Randolph Scott and James Flavin.

Ella Raines and Randolph Scott.

Corvette K-225 is the story of one such ship and its adventures in crossing from Halifax, Nova Scotia, to the British Isles. Rossen's picture is almost documentary in style and vividly shows the dangers and tensions of life on a corvette under duty, including the dreadful weather in winter, when ferocious storms lash the small craft with huge, vicious waves that drench the crew. When not pitching and tossing in wallowing seas, the sailors are subject to bombardment from the air and torpedo attack from under the sea.

A thin fictional yarn keeps *Corvette K-225* from being a pure photographic war record. Lieutenant Commander MacClain (Randolph Scott) is a tough, experienced corvette captain assigned a rather cocky fledging officer (James Brown), who is the brother of MacClain's girlfriend (Ella Raines). MacClain's problem is to whip the young man into shape without alienating his sister. Randolph Scott is particularly good as the skipper, but the real credit for the film belongs to Richard Rossen, whose close contact with his material clearly left him with a resolve to treat it realistically and respectfully.

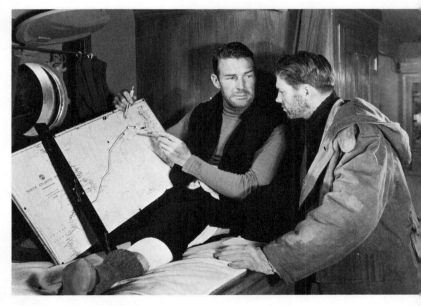

Randolph Scott and James Brown.

99

Carmen Miranda, the Lady in the Tutti-Frutti Hat.

The Gang's All Here

1943

A 20th Century-Fox Production; produced by William LeBaron; directed by Busby Berkeley; screenplay by Walter Bullock, based on a story by Nancy Wintner, George Root, and Tom Bridges; photographed in Technicolor by Edward Cronjager; songs by Harry Warren and Leo Robin; musical direction by Alfred Newman; running time, 103 minutes.

Cast: Alice Faye (*Eadie*), Carmen Miranda (*Rosita*), Phil Baker (*himself*), Benny Goodman (*himself*), Eugene Pallette (*Mr. Mason, Sr.*), Charlotte Greenwood (*Mrs. Peyson Potter*), Edward Everett Horton (*Peyson Potter*), Tony DeMarco (*himself*), James Ellison (*Andy Mason*), Sheila Ryan (*Vivian*), Dave Willock (*Sergeant Casey*), Miriam Lavelle (*Specialty Dancer*).

Alice Faye.

Busby Berkeley's fame rests largely on the gargantuan musicals he did for Warners in the 1930s. When they went out of fashion he took to doing less fantastic and slightly more believable pictures for MGM. However, in 1943 he slipped back a decade and refurbished his old tricks for 20th Century-Fox in *The Gang's All Here*. This time he had the advantage of advanced camera equipment and the stunning addition of rich, glowing Technicolor.

Berkeley here summarized his whole weird and wonderful contribution to the art of the movie musical, and by beautiful coincidence his composer was Harry Warren, the same man who had supplied the music for Berkeley's best Warners productions. Warren and lyricist Leo Robin came up with half a dozen songs to give Berkeley scope for his imagination. Two of them are ballads for Alice Faye—"A Journey to a Star" and "No Love, No Nothing"— and for the zesty Carmen Miranda they supplied the highly appropriate "The Lady in the Tutti-frutti Hat."

Benny Goodman and his band play "Paducah" and "Minnie's in the Money," and there are two elaborate production numbers, "You Discover You're in New York," in which an ocean liner from South America disgorges hordes of singing and dancing visitors, and "The Polka Dot Polka."

The plot is the least of the film's assets. It deals with an army sergeant (James Ellison) who falls for a nightclub singer (Faye) but doesn't tell her that he is the son of wealthy, society people or that he has a fiancée (Sheila Ryan), a girl in his own money bracket whom he has known since childhood. Faye turns out to be more interested in a show business career than in Ellison, so the way is cleared for Ellison and Ryan. The girl invites the entire cast of a Manhattan nightclub to perform at the home of her parents (Edward Everett Horton and Charlotte Greenwood), and it is there that the personal issues are settled. It is also there that some incredible production numbers are staged, including a ballet derived from "The Polka Dot Polka," involving breathtaking kaleidoscopic effects.

Considered par for the course at the time, and subsequently forgotten, *The Gang's All Here* was revived and widely shown in 1971, when it became apparent that the film was a testament to Busby Berkeley's genius for staging dance compositions in elaborate and continuously mobile settings, with fluid camera movements. This was the high-water mark in his career.

Charlotte Greenwood, Edward Everett Horton and Carmen Miranda.

Elsa Lanchester, Roddy McDowall and Donald Crisp.

Lassie Come Home

1943

An MGM Production; produced by Samuel Marx; directed by Fred M. Wilcox; screenplay by Hugo Butler, based on the novel by Eric Knight; photographed in Technicolor by Leonard Smith; musical score by Daniele Amfitheatrof; running time, 88 minutes.

Cast: Roddy McDowall (*Joe Carraclough*), Donald Crisp (*Sam Carraclough*), Edmund Gwenn (*Rowlie*), Dame May Whitty (*Dolly*), Nigel Bruce (*Duke of Rudling*), Elsa Lanchester (*Mrs. Carraclough*), Elizabeth Taylor (*Priscilla*), J. Patrick O'Malley (*Hynes*), Ben Webster (*Dan'l Fadden*), Alec Craig (*Snickers*), John Rogers (*Buckles*), Arthur Shields (*Jock*), Alan Napier (*Andrew*), Roy Parry (*Butcher*).

Several sequels to *Lassie Come Home*, plus a long-running television series, have dulled the memory of the original film. This is a pity, because *Lassie Come Home* is a fine film, well written and acted, and especially well photographed in color by

Elizabeth Taylor, Elsa Lanchester, Donald Crisp and Nigel Bruce.

Leonard Smith in beautiful pastoral settings. Respect is also due for the performance of Lassie, a collie then two years old, chosen from among hundreds of tested dogs.

Rudd Weatherwax, who bought the dog for ten dollars as a pup, taught Lassie to swim rivers, climb mountains, fight other dogs and human thugs, and make her way through rain and snow as the story required. Although the story was set in England and Scotland, the company filmed on locations in the lake and mountain region of interior Washington, at the rugged California coast at Monterey, and on the swift San Joaquin River. Unlike the human actors, Lassie was never heard to complain.

The story is one of devotion between a young boy and his dog. Joe (Roddy McDowall) and Lassie are constant companions until the day his parents (Donald Crisp and Elsa Lanchester) regretfully tell him that they have had to sell the dog for much-needed money. The new owner, the Duke of Rudling (Nigel Bruce), has so much trouble keeping Lassie in his kennels and away from the boy that he takes the dog to his estate in Scotland, to train her for showing. But Lassie breaks away from her trainer and heads south.

She makes her way across miles of rough, empty countryside, through foul weather and attacks from other animals. She is shot by a sheep farmer and nursed back to health by a kindly old couple, but once she is well she takes up her trek.

Eventually she arrives back in the village of Greenal Bridge, Yorkshire, and proceeds to her former home. At four in the afternoon, as always, she goes to the school to meet Joe. Neither his parents nor the Duke have the heart to come between the boy and the dog again.

Before making this film fourteen-year-old Roddy McDowall had scored such a hit as a horse-loving boy in *My Friend Flicka* that MGM considered no other youngster for the lead in *Lassie Come Home.* Certainly McDowall was a very appealing and convincing youngster, and without that appeal and conviction his roles in *Flicka* and *Lassie* might have become ludicrous. Only the jaundiced can look at these films and fail to be impressed with their quality.

103

The Lodger

Laird Cregar and Merle Oberon.

Sara Allgood and Laird Cregar.

George Sanders, Merle Oberon and Frederick Worlock.

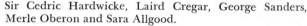

Sir Cedric Hardwicke, Laird Cregar, George Sanders, Merle Oberon and Sara Allgood.

1944

A 20th Century-Fox Production; produced by Robert Bassler; directed by John Brahm; screenplay by Barre Lyndon, based on the novel by Marie Belloc-Lowndes; photographed by Lucien Ballard; musical score by Hugo Friedhofer; running time, 84 minutes.

Cast: Merle Oberon (*Kitty*), George Sanders (*John Warrick*), Laird Cregar (*the Lodger*), Sir Cedric Hardwicke (*Robert Burton*), Sara Allgood (*Ellen*), Aubrey Mather (*Superintendent Sutherland*), Queenie Leonard (*Daisy*), Doris Lloyd (*Jennie*), David Clyde (*Sergeant Bates*), Helena Pickard (*Anne Rowley*), Lumsden Hare (*Doctor Sheridan*), Frederic Worlock (*Sir Edward*), Olaf Hytten (*Harris*), Colin Campbell (*Harold*), Harold De Becker (*Charlie*).

Marie Belloc-Lowndes's novel *The Lodger* made quite an impact in 1913 because not only was it based on the hideous crimes of Jack the Ripper, but it probed the psychology of crime, a new tack at that time. The notorious killer terrorized the Whitechapel district of London in the late 1880s, and since the Ripper was never apprehended Mrs. Belloc-Lowndes allowed herself imaginative scope in dealing with his personality and the fear he caused.

In making the film, Fox producers also allowed themselves scope, drenching the screen in swirling fog and filling the damp night air with the screams of butchered victims. As the pathological murderer, Laird Cregar romped melodramatically through the film, aided by Lucien Ballard's fluid photography and an eerie, pulsating score by Hugo Friedhofer.

And as with many other London-set movies, Fox culled the cast from Hollywood's plentiful colony of British actors.

The lodger of the title is a glum and lonely individual looking for accommodation. A genteel couple, Mr. and Mrs. Robert Burton (Sir Cedric Hardwicke and Sara Allgood), rent a room to him, little realizing that they are endangering the life of their daughter Kitty (Merle Oberon), who is an entertainer. Their lodger is a man who kills actresses because one once caused grief to his brother. Kitty comes to suspect that the lodger is the man bringing terror to the neighborhood and that she is on his list. She is saved by a Scotland Yard inspector (George Sanders), a pioneer in the science of criminology. The killer meets his end after an exciting chase through a theater, and he crashes through a window into the Thames, an ending at variance with the Belloc-Lowndes novel.

Merle Oberon appears to advantage in *The Lodger,* performing nicely in two music-hall sequences and showing understandable concern about the attention paid her by the gentleman lodging in her home. Laird Cregar was criticized at the time for overdoing the dramatics of his juicy role, and yet his presence gives the film its compelling quality. This large and distinctive actor lived to make only one more film, *Hangover Square,* which also required him to be a pathological character in old foggy London. Desperate to reduce his weight from three hundred pounds so that he could play more romantic parts, Cregar wrecked his health. He died of a heart attack in 1944, a mere twenty-eight years old, a shocking loss of talent to Hollywood.

Jane Eyre

1944

A 20th Century-Fox Production; produced by William Goetz; directed by Robert Stevenson; screenplay by Aldous Huxley, Robert Stevenson, and John Houseman, based on the book by Charlotte Brontë; photographed by George Barnes; musical score by Bernard Herrmann; running time, 96 minutes.

Cast: Orson Welles (*Edward Rochester*), Joan Fontaine (*Jane Eyre*), Margaret O'Brien (*Adele Varens*), Peggy Ann Garner (*Jane as a child*), John Sutton (*Doctor Rivers*), Sara Allgood (*Bessie*), Henry Daniell (*Brocklehurst*), Agnes Moorehead (*Mrs. Reed*), Aubrey Mather (*Colonel Dent*), Edith Barrett (*Mrs. Fairfax*), Barbara Everest (*Lady Ingram*), Hilary Brooke (*Blanche Ingram*), Ethel Griffies (*Grace Poole*), Mae Marsh (*Leah*), Yorke Sherwood (*Beadle*), John Abbot (*Mason*), Ronald Harris (*John*).

106

Peggy Ann Garner (on the stool) and Henry Daniell (pointing).

Joan Fontaine and Orson Welles.

Orson Welles, Joan Fontaine and John Abbott.

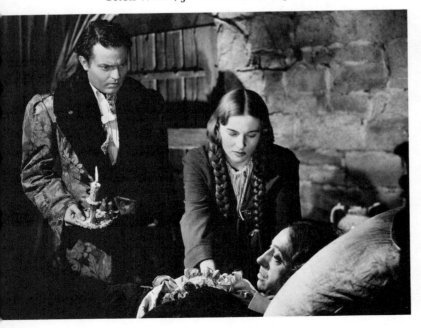

Charlotte Brontë's darkly romantic melodrama *Jane Eyre* stood no chance of escaping moviemakers. It was filmed in several silent versions, and the first sound version was made in 1934, with Virginia Bruce and Colin Clive. More recently it was impressively acted by George C. Scott and Susannah York, with the advantage of being photographed in color on suitably bleak British locations. But even the most recent version lacks the quality of the one made entirely on 20th Century-Fox sound stages in 1943. This one benefited from the presence of Orson Welles as Mr. Rochester, and Welles clearly affected the production values—this is a Kane-like Rochester and his Thornfield manorhouse smacks of the arrogant grandeur of Xanadu. Aldous Huxley and John Houseman shared the screenplay credit with director Robert Stevenson, but it is safe to assume that they respected Welles's opinions and ideas.

However, the attention paid Orson Welles should not obscure Joan Fontaine's delicate portrayal of the title role. Fontaine here continued her winning streak of the early forties. As in *Rebecca,* she was again required to be shy and demure and yet emerge triumphant at the end.

Stevenson's picture is a literate treatment of the familiar Brontë material—the story of an orphaned girl who grows up in a boarding school and secures a position as a governess in the home of the wealthy but tormented Edward Rochester. She and Rochester come to love each other, but their intended marriage is interrupted by the revelation that Rochester already has a wife, a madwoman locked away in the attic. Jane flees from Thornfield and suffers privations in making her living, but she one day senses a need to return to Thornfield. She finds the house gutted by fire, the mad wife consumed in the holocaust, and Rochester blinded by it. Jane and the pitifully subdued master are now free to find their happiness together.

This is a *Jane Eyre* of splendid cinematic style, strikingly photographed by George Barnes and scored by the masterly Bernard Herrmann, the composer who had supplied music for Welles's *Citizen Kane* and *The Magnificent Ambersons* and for many of his radio dramas. Some critics find Welles's Rochester somewhat overripe, but it is nonetheless a commanding performance, gently and skillfully matched by Miss Fontaine's Jane. The acting of a fine cast helps overcome the realization that the original material is really little more than schoolgirlish Victorian hokum.

To the left of Crosby — Fortunio Bonanova, Risë Stevens and Frank McHugh.

Going My Way

1944

A Paramount Production; produced and directed by Leo McCarey; screenplay by Frank Butler and Frank Cavett, based on a story by Leo McCarey; photographed by Lionel Lindon; songs by Johnny Burke and Jimmy Van Heusen; musical direction by Robert Emmett Dolan; running time, 130 minutes.

Cast: Bing Crosby (*Father O'Malley*), Risë Stevens (*Genevieve Linden*), Barry Fitzgerald (*Father Fitzgibbon*), Frank McHugh (*Father Timothy O'Dowd*), James Brown (*Ted Haines*), Gene Lockhart (*Haines, Sr.*), Jean Heather (*Carol James*), Porter Hall (*Mr. Belknap*), Fortunio Bonanova (*Tomaso Bozzani*), Eily Malyon (*Mrs. Carmody*), the Robert Mitchell Boychoir (*themselves*).

109

Bing Crosby and Barry Fitzgerald.

Barry Fitzgerald, Risë Stevens and Bing Crosby.

Frank McHugh, Barry Fitzgerald, Bing Crosby and
Gene Lockhart.

It was Gary Cooper who handed Bing Crosby the
Oscar for his performance as a Catholic priest in
Going My Way, an excellent choice because both
actors had much in common. Both appeared not to
act on the screen, to be playing themselves, and as
any actor knows this is quite an accomplishment.
Crosby is modest about this rare ability to be seemingly at ease in front of the cameras, and in this
film he claims he was lucky to have had Leo
McCarey "take me by the hand and lead me
through the picture."

The shrewd McCarey, who dreamed up the
whole project, knew what he was doing in selecting
Crosby for the part. The veteran crooner's easygoing manner masks his shrewdness, and as Father
O'Malley he left no doubt that this was a firm-
minded churchman.

Father O'Malley is sent to rehabilitate a run-
down parish administered by an old priest, Father
Fitzgibbon (Barry Fitzgerald). The old church,
built and presided over for the past forty-five years
by Fitzgibbon, is much in debt and in need of
repair. O'Malley's assignment is to quietly supplant
the old priest without his being aware of it.

O'Malley's modern methods and manners irritate
Fitzgibbon, who complains to his superiors and

learns the truth of the situation. In time Fitzgibbon
comes to like and appreciate O'Malley, although
the crotchety old fellow never shows it.

O'Malley forms a boys' choir, and to help sell a
song he has written, he enlists the aid of an opera
star (Risë Stevens). He hopes the sale will bring in
money for his church and its debts, which it does.

But the church burns down, and even more
money is needed to build a new one. O'Malley's
winning personality enlists the altruism of a local
builder and brings the community together in pur-
pose and harmony. Then, with his mission successful, O'Malley packs his bags and moves on.

According to Leo McCarey the film was based on
incidents in the career of an actual priest.

Going My Way was a winner in critical acclaim
and in wide popularity, and at the Academy
Awards it did a landslide business. Oscars went to
the film, to Crosby, to McCarey as best director, to
Barry Fitzgerald, and to Johnny Burke and Jimmy
Van Heusen for writing "Swinging on a Star."
Crosby also sang their title song and "The Day
after Forever," as well as an old Irish ballad, "Too-
ra-loo-ra-loo-ra." Even with the familiarity of his
singing, Crosby managed to be completely convincing as Father O'Malley.

110

Barbara Stanwyck, Tom Powers and Fred MacMurray.

Double Indemnity

1944

A Paramount Production; produced by Joseph Sistrom; directed by Billy Wilder; screenplay by Billy Wilder and Raymond Chandler, based on the story by James M. Cain; photographed by John F. Seitz; musical score by Miklos Rozsa; running time, 107 minutes.

Cast: Fred MacMurray (*Walter Neff*), Barbara Stanwyck (*Phyllis Dietrichson*), Edward G. Robinson (*Barton Keyes*), Porter Hall (*Mr. Jackson*), Jean Heather (*Lola Dietrichson*), Tom Powers (*Mr. Dietrichson*), Byron Barr (*Nino Zachette*), Richard Gaines (*Mr. Norton*), Fortunio Bonanova (*Sam Gorlopis*), John Philliber (*Joe Pete*).

111

Fred MacMurray and Edward G. Robinson.

Barbara Stanwyck, Fred MacMurray and Edward G. Robinson.

Double Indemnity was the first film by Billy Wilder that fully revealed his talent as a filmmaker and showed his mordantly humorous view of mankind. He had long been a noted scriptwriter, but as a director he had made only *The Major and the Minor* (1942) and *Five Graves to Cairo,* neither of which prepared Hollywood for the searingly bleak drama of *Double Indemnity.*

Wilder and the noted crime-fiction writer Raymond Chandler expanded James M. Cain's magazine story, based on a New York murder case of 1927 in which a wife and her lover killed her husband to gain his insurance money. Wilder set his story in Los Angeles. He used many locations in the city and avoided any attempt to glamorize his settings. There is nothing appealing about the characters or their surroundings, and yet the film has a strangely compelling quality, rather like fascinating reptiles destroying each other.

The picture opens on a car weaving its way through city streets at night. Walter Neff (Fred MacMurray) staggers to his insurance office suffering from a bullet wound. He sits at his desk and records a story for the benefit of his investigating colleague, Barton Keyes (Edward G. Robinson). It is a confession in which Neff tells how he and Phyllis Dietrichson (Barbara Stanwyck) devised a scheme to kill her husband (Tom Powers) and defraud the insurance company of a hefty policy. They place the husband's body on railroad tracks and cleverly make his death appear the result of an accident.

The plan might have worked, but Neff comes to realize that he has been duped by this vicious woman, and he shoots her. The story ends with Neff in the gas chamber and his friend Keyes wiser with the knowledge that he is not the infallible insurance investigator he had believed himself.

Wilder touches give *Double Indemnity* its style —its starkness and its uncompromising treatment of dark, cold material. Its keynote is dry suspense. Fred MacMurray resisted playing the role, feeling that it was counter to his light image, but Wilder prevailed. The casual, affable MacMurray image makes the role all the more chilling. However, the image of Barbara Stanwyck marks this picture most indelibly. With a white wig and usually dressed in white costumes, she here seems a beautiful wraith, cold and bloodless, luring men with a faintly evil smile. Truly a remarkable performance.

Ingrid Bergman and Charles Boyer.

Gaslight

1944

An MGM Production; produced by Arthur Hornblow, Jr.; directed by George Cukor; screenplay by John Van Druten, Walter Reisch, and John L. Balderston, based on the play *Angel Street*, by Patrick Hamilton; photographed by Joseph Ruttenberg; musical score by Bronislau Kaper; running time, 114 minutes.

Cast: Charles Boyer (*Gregory Anton*), Ingrid Bergman (*Paula Alquist*), Joseph Cotten (*Brian Cameron*), Dame May Whitty (*Miss Thwaites*), Angela Lansbury (*Nancy Oliver*), Barbara Everest (*Elizabeth Tompkins*), Emil Rameau (*Mario Gardi*), Edmund Breon (*General Huddelston*), Halliwell Hobbes (*Mr. Mufflin*), Tom Stevenson (*Williams*), Heather Thatcher (*Lady Dalroy*), Lawrence Grossmith (*Lord Dalroy*).

Joseph Cotten, Charles Boyer and Ingrid Bergman.

When MGM decided to make *Gaslight,* they acquired the negative of the British film of the same title, based on the same play, and withdrew it from circulation. In time, the 1940 British film mysteriously gained a reputation as a lost masterpiece, vastly superior to the Hollywood product.

An impartial viewing of the two films (several prints of the British film are in circulation among film societies) deflates the legend. The films are different stylistically, and each has qualities of its own. The British picture, with Anton Walbrook and Diana Wynyard, stays close to Patrick Hamilton's stage play and is small scale and intimate. The MGM version is vastly superior in production values, considerably altered and developed to make plausible the European accents of Charles Boyer and Ingrid Bergman, and consequently runs twenty-six minutes longer than the British version.

The screenplay by John Van Druten, Walter Reisch, and John L. Balderston establishes the villainous husband as a pianist, Gregory Anton (Boyer), who accompanies Paula Alquist (Bergman) as she studies singing in Italy. He courts and marries her and persuades her against her wishes to return to live in a house in London left to her by her aunt, the famous opera star Alice Alquist, murdered in the house a few years previously.

Anton, a very charming, cool, and calculating fellow, needs to get back to the house because he is the murderer, but he failed to achieve the object of the murder—to steal the star's valuable collection of jewels. He seals off the upper story of the house, ostensibly to shield his wife from the area she fears, but enters it at night from the empty house next door and spends hours looking for the gems. Meanwhile he subtly campaigns to mentally derange his wife, almost convincing her that she is in need of commitment.

Her sanity is saved, and Anton's plans thwarted, by the sympathy and investigations of a detective, Brian Cameron (Joseph Cotten). The captured Anton begs his wife's help in escaping, but his charm no longer works on her. The once doting, sweet-natured Paula now has the strength to turn away from him.

This *Gaslight* is a textbook example of MGM expertise at the peak of that studio's power. The brilliant acting of Boyer and Bergman and George Cukor's artful direction are backed by superb sets, decor, and costumes, the subtle scoring of Bronislau Kaper, and the exceptionally clear and dramatically lit photography of Joseph Ruttenberg.

115

Ingrid Bergman, Angela Lansbury and Charles Boyer.

Fredric March, John Carradine and Alan Hale.

The Adventures of Mark Twain

1944

A Warner Bros. Production; produced by Jesse L. Lasky; directed by Irving Rapper; screenplay by Alan LeMay, adapted by Alan LeMay and Harold M. Sherman from biographical material owned by the Mark Twain Company; photographed by Sol Polito, Laurence Butler, Edwin Linden, Don Siegel, and James Leicester; musical score by Max Steiner; running time, 130 minutes.

Cast: Fredric March (*Samuel Clemens/Mark Twain*), Alexis Smith (*Olivia Langdon*), Donald Crisp (*J. B. Pond*), Alan Hale (*Steve Gillis*), C. Aubrey Smith (*Oxford Chancellor*), John Carradine (*Bret Harte*), William Henry (*Charles Langdon*), Robert Barrat (*Horace E. Bixby*), Walter Hampden (*Jervis Langdon*), Joyce Reynolds (*Clara Clemens*), Whitford Kane (*Joe Goodwin*), Percy Kilbride (*Billings*), Nana Bryant (*Mrs. Langdon*), Jackie Brown (*Sam at twelve*), Dickie Jones (*Sam at fifteen*), Russell Gleason (*Orrin Clemens*), Joseph Crehan (*General Grant*), Douglas Wood (*William Dean Howells*).

Hollywood biographies of famed American musical, literary, and historical figures—a favorite film avenue of the forties—were notably high handed in distorting facts. The producers argued that they were in the business of dispensing entertainment. This cavalier attitude is most apparent in *The Adventures of Mark Twain,* a very long, sprawling account of the witty storyteller from Hannibal, Missouri, whose long life (1835–1910) matched the spirit and growth of his country.

What saves this well-mounted movie is the splendid performance of Fredric March, who in the episodes showing Twain as an old man achieves a remarkable portrayal. March had been a major

116

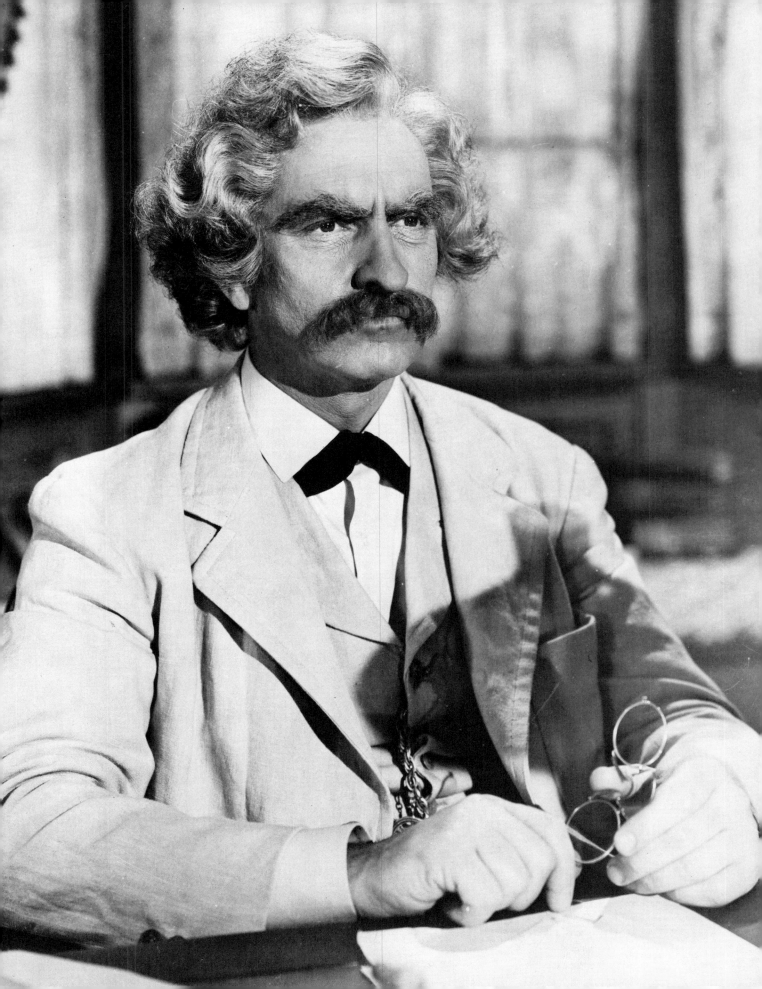

movie star of the thirties, but as he entered his middle age he decided to divide his time between films and the stage. Unlike many actors who attempt this split-level career, March was conspicuously successful. Whether in front of an audience or the cameras, March was a dedicated and convincing actor.

The trouble with this film is its subject. Samuel Clemens lived seventy-five busy years and turned out an enormous quantity of work—and Warners tried to cover it all. It shows his early years, his adventures as a Mississippi riverboat man, his wanderings to the wild West, his involvement in California gold mining, his experience as a newspaper reporter and his success writing the famous story about the jumping frogs.

The film then shows Twain as a writer of growing stature, courting and winning the well-bred Olivia Langdon (Alexis Smith), against the wishes of her parents, and gradually becoming a world figure and a world traveler. It also touches upon some of Twain's sadder episodes—his bankruptcy following his publishing disasters and his near exhaustion in working to clear his debts.

The film derives entertainment from parading Twain's epigrams and comments on humankind, particularly in the later years when he became a kind of performing pundit.

The Adventures of Mark Twain are too many, and the picture is forced to montage too much of his life. However, there is much to amuse and enlighten in this film, and if it serves to inspire study of the life and times of Samuel Clemens, all criticisms can be dismissed. Additionally, it is a showcase for the civilized talents of Fredric March.

Fredric March and Alexis Smith.

118

June Allyson and Gloria De Haven.

Two Girls and a Sailor

1944

An MGM Production; produced by Joe Pasternak; directed by Richard Thorpe; screenplay by Richard Connell and Gladys Lehman; photographed by Robert Surtees; musical direction by George Stoll; running time, 124 minutes.

Cast: Van Johnson (*John Dyckman Brown III*), June Allyson (*Patsy Deyo*), Gloria De Haven (*Jean Deyo*), Jimmy Durante (*Billy Kipp*), Tom Drake (*Frank Miller*), Henry Stephenson (*John Dyckman Brown I*), Henry O'Neill (*John Dyckman Brown II*), Ben Blue (*Ben*), Carlos Ramirez (*Carlos*), Frank Sully (*Private Adams*), Donald Meek (*Mr. Nizby*), Frank Jenks (*Dick Deyo*), Jose Iturbi, Gracie Allen, Lena Horne, Albert Coates, Amparo Navarro, Virginia O'Brien, the Wilde twins, Harry James and his band, Helen Forrest, Xavier Cugat and his band, Lina Romay (*themselves*).

When MGM bought the screen rights to the Broadway musical *Best Foot Forward,* they brought a few members of the original cast to appear in the film version. Among them was June Allyson. Her pert personality, appealingly husky voice, and smiling eyes made an immediate hit, and she was placed under contract. After she played bits in *Girl Crazy, As Thousands Cheer* (1943), and *Meet the People,* during the course of which she met and married Dick Powell, the studio gambled on giving her the lead in *Two Girls and a Sailor,* backing her with an enormous array of famous guest stars. The resultant popularity locked her into the MGM folds for the next ten years.

This is a fairly typical wartime Metro musical. Few other studios had the wherewithal to load a picture with quite as many names as this. Even if the slim plot and all the nonmusical sequences were pulled from it, what remains would make an hour of entertainment by topnotch performers.

The plot concerns a pair of sisters, Patsy (Allyson) and Jean (Gloria De Haven), who perform together as entertainers. They open their homes to servicemen as a kind of private USO, and they are surprised to find that their efforts are rewarded by

Dream Sequence — Jimmy Durante, Donald Meek, June Allyson and Van Johnson.

generous donations and the gratis services of famous performers.

It turns out that one of their guests, a young sailor (Van Johnson), is superwealthy and supplying their every need. Both sisters fall in love with him, but there is never any doubt of the outcome. Patsy, the practical but sweet older sister, almost a mother to the capricious Jean, is the winner, but Jean happily ends up in the arms of a handsome Texas sergeant (Tom Drake).

The musical bill of fare includes the bands of Harry James and Xavier Cugat, and Jose Iturbi and

his sister Amparo playing "The Ritual Fire Dance." Pianism of another kind is supplied by Gracie Allen and her piano concerto for one finger, and the lovable Jimmy Durante bats out his "Inka Dinka Doo." Among the songs are "Paper Moon," magnificently sung by Lena Horne, and "Take It Easy," sung deadpan by Virginia O'Brien. The two female stars also perform, and June Allyson's "Young Man with a Horn," backed by Harry James, is a genuine highlight and an added reason for her emergence in this bright and breezy picture as a performer taking the public by storm.

120

Van Johnson, June Allyson, Jimmy
Durante and Ben Blue.

Van Johnson, June Allyson and Gloria De Haven.

George Sanders and Linda Darnell.

Summer Storm

1944

A United Artists Production; produced by Seymour Nebenzel; directed by Douglas Sirk; screenplay by Rowland Lee, based on *The Shooting Party*, by Anton Chekhov; photographed by Archie M. Stout; musical score by Karl Hajos; running time, 106 minutes.

Cast: George Sanders (*Fedor Michailovitch Petroff*), Linda Darnell (*Olga Urbenin*), Anna Lee (*Nadina*), Edward Everett Horton (*Count Volsky*), Hugo Haas (*Urbenin*), Lori Lahner (*Clara*), John Philhber (*Polycarp*), Sig Rumann (*Kuzma*), Andre Charlot (*Mr. Kalenin*), Mary Servoss (*Mrs. Kalenini*), John Abbott (*Lunin*), Robert Greig (*Gregory*), Nina Koschetz (*Gypsy Singer*), Paul Hurst (*Gendarme*), Charles Trowbridge (*Doctor*).

Summer Storm was an unlikely film to be produced in Hollywood in 1944. Russian classical literature was not considered the stuff of commercial movies, and this film came about as the result of determination on the part of the group who wanted to make it. This first Hollywood effort at filming a Chekhov tale, completed for $360,000, gave Linda Darnell and Edward Everett Horton two of the best roles in their careers. It allowed Darnell to show that she had more ability than her previous pictures had suggested, and here the severely type-cast Horton, almost always the gentle buffoon, managed to give a subtle performance as a decadent nobleman, hiding despair behind a gay front.

Rowland Lee's excellent script, based on Chekhov's *The Shooting Party*, was directed by Douglas Sirk, a German who made a strong first impression in Hollywood in 1943 with *Hitler's Madman*, a searing account of Heydrich, the Nazi chieftain who liquidated the Czech village of Lidice. Sirk's career as a director with a strong, personal style has received recognition in recent years, and *Summer Storm,* never impressive as a box-office winner, is now regarded as one of Hollywood's great "little" pictures.

Set in Russia in the years just before the revolution it deals with a Carmen-like peasant beauty, Olga (Darnell), and her effect on the various men she uses in her quest for social advancement. She marries a middle-aged farmer (Hugo Haas), to escape her father, and the poor husband patiently endures her indiscretions.

Olga's main victim becomes an aristocratic judge (George Sanders), who casts aside his fiancée (Anna Lee) and ruins his career in his passion for the voluptuous but shallow Olga. Eventually he realizes her worthlessness and kills her. He is killed while trying to escape from the police.

Summer Storm was a highlight in George Sanders' career, and he understood the role perfectly. Despite his British name and accent, Sanders was born into the Russian upper-milieu society, and in *The Memoirs of a Professional Cad* he wrote amusingly about the hedonism and the inevitable decline of St. Petersburg's monied classes. That kind of insight, plus good performances and production values, made *Summer Storm* a small, rare gem of a film for its time and place.

Edward Everett Horton and Linda Darnell.

Linda Darnell and George Sanders.

Linda Darnell and Edward Everett Horton.

Meet Me in St. Louis

1944

An MGM Production; produced by Arthur Freed; directed by Vincente Minnelli; screenplay by Irving Becher and Fred F. Finklehoffe, based on a story by Sally Benson; photographed in Technicolor by George Folsey; songs by Ralph Blane and Hugh Martin; musical direction by George Stoll; running time, 113 minutes.

Cast: Judy Garland (*Esther Smith*), Margaret O'Brien (*Tootie*), Mary Astor (*Mrs. Smith*), Lucille Bremer (*Rose Smith*), June Lockhart (*Lucille Ballard*), Tom Drake (*John Truett*), Marjorie Main (*Katie*), Harry Davenport (*Grandpa*), Leon Ames (*Alonzo Smith*), Henry Daniels, Jr. (*Lon Smith, Jr.*), Joan Carroll (*Agnes Smith*), Hugh Marlowe (*Colonel Darly*), Robert Sully (*Warren Sheffield*), Chill Wills (*Mr. Neely*).

The art of the movie musical took a giant step forward with *Meet Me in St. Louis,* thanks largely to the direction of Vincente Minnelli. A man of taste and sensitivity, Minnelli spent the early years of his career as a designer and art director for the stage. This is an idealized and sentimental piece of Americana, but nothing about it is false or mawkish.

The picture is set in St. Louis, Missouri, in 1903, the year before the World's Fair, and tells of a nice middle-class family, the Smiths. Their pleasant and secure lives become ruffled when it seems likely that father (Leon Ames) will be transferred to New York for business reasons, taking the family with him and causing them to leave the house and the city they love. When he realizes the anguish the move will bring his children, the stern but loving parent changes his mind.

There is very little plot in *Meet Me in St. Louis,* and it doesn't need one. It's a delightful string of family incidents and warm characterizations, and its songs, mostly by Ralph Blane and Hugh Martin, with a few oldies mixed in for good measure, practically tell the tale. The title song is sung by the whole family in their home; father and mother (Mary Astor) sit at the piano and sing their affection for one another, "You and I"; Esther (Judy

Garland) and little sister Tootie (Margaret O'Brien) entertain the family with "Under the Bamboo Tree"; Esther expresses her yearning about "The Boy Next Door" and her happiness with the world in "The Trolley Song"; the family and their guests dance and sing to "Skip to My Lou"; and Esther sings to her boyfriend "Over the Banisters" and consoles Tootie, depressed because she fears this will be her last Yuletide in St. Louis, with "Have Yourself a Merry Little Christmas."

The MGM art department excelled in this film.

Their work graces the eye with pleasing sets exquisitely color photographed by George Folsey. But the master hand belongs to Minnelli, who obviously shared the public's fascination with the lovely twenty-two-year-old Judy Garland, radiant with her girlish warmth and clear, vibrant voice. She and Minnelli were married a year later, and even though the marriage came to an end she always claimed this as the favorite of her movies and fully credited Minnelli for its excellence.

Leon Ames, Judy Garland, Harry Davenport, Lucille Bremer, Henry Daniels, Jr., Joan Carroll and Mary Astor.

Judy Garland, Lucille Bremer and Tom Drake.

June Lockhart, Henry Daniels, Jr., Harry Davenport and Judy Garland.

126

Joan Carroll, Judy Garland, Margaret O'Brien and Lucille Bremer.

Gene Tierney and Dana Andrews.

Laura

1944

A 20th Century-Fox Production; produced and directed by Otto Preminger; screenplay by Jay Dratler, Samuel Hoffenstein, and Betty Reinhardt, based on the novel by Vera Casparay; photographed by Joseph La Shelle; musical score by David Raksin; running time, 88 minutes.

Cast: Gene Tierney (*Laura Hunt*), Dana Andrews (*Mark McPherson*), Clifton Webb (*Waldo Lydecker*), Vincent Price (*Shelby Carpenter*), Judith Anderson (*Anne Treadwell*), Dorothy Adams (*Bessie Clary*), James Flavin (*McAvity*), Clyde Fillmore (*Bullitt*), Ralph Dunn (*Fred Callahan*), Grant Mitchell (*Corey*), Kathleen Howard (*Louise*).

Laura belongs to that large body of films which emerged as excellent in spite of the conditions under which they were made. Darryl F. Zanuck

assigned Otto Preminger to produce the picture, but several directors turned down the script. Rouben Mamoulian finally accepted it, but several weeks into the filming both Preminger and Zanuck decided that they didn't like Mamoulian's treatment and dismissed him. Zanuck then told Preminger to direct the film himself.

When the shooting was completed, more tribulations dogged the production. Various Fox executives persuaded Zanuck that the final sequences should be rewritten and filmed again. The result was so muddled that Zanuck instructed Preminger to proceed with his original version. In this form *Laura* became a box-office winner and gradually acquired its reputation as one of the most stylish and witty murder mysteries ever filmed. It established Preminger as a director and brought Clifton Webb to prominence after a long career on the stage as a dancer and actor.

Clifton Webb and Dana Andrews.

Clifton Webb and Gene Tierney.

Webb was part of the trauma of *Laura*—the Fox officers considered him too grandly epicene to be acceptable to movie audiences, but Preminger insisted on using him, and rightly so. Webb's unforgettable portrayal of the cultured, bitchy intellectual Waldo Lydecker launched him on a decade of stardom.

The lovely girl of the title (Gene Tierney) is thought to have been murdered, since a body like hers, with the face obliterated by a shotgun blast, was found outside her apartment. Detective Mark McPherson (Dana Andrews) investigates. He suspects Waldo Lydecker, but Laura's weak, playboyish fiancé, Shelby Carpenter (Vincent Price), appears the more likely culprit.

It evolves that the corpse is that of a model with whom Carpenter had been having an affair and that Lydecker killed the girl, assuming that she was Laura. The madly jealous Lydecker had been so attached to Laura that he vowed she should never belong to anyone else.

The man who finally gets Laura is the detective, who falls in love with her portrait and is amazed and relieved when she proves to be alive.

One of the major assets of this perfectly paced and acted picture is the haunting score by David Raksin. The main theme immediately caught the public fancy and, with a lyric added by Johnny Mercer, remains a classic popular song. Preminger had wanted to use Ellington's "Sophisticated Lady" as the theme, but fortunately Raksin had other ideas. On a Friday Preminger gave Raksin until Monday to come up with his own theme. The result is a perfect example of the effectiveness of appropriate film scoring.

Vincent Price, Judith Anderson, Gene Tierney and Clifton Webb.

Vincent Price, Dana Andrews and Gene Tierney.

Mickey Rooney and Elizabeth Taylor.

National Velvet

1945

An MGM Production; produced by Pandro S. Berman; directed by Clarence Brown; screenplay by Theodore Reeves and Helen Deutsch, based on the novel by Enid Bagnold; photographed in Technicolor by Leonard Smith; musical score by Herbert Stothart; running time, 125 minutes.

Cast: Mickey Rooney (*Mi Taylor*), Donald Crisp (*Mr. Brown*), Elizabeth Taylor (*Velvet Brown*), Anne Revere (*Mrs. Brown*), Angela Lansbury (*Edwina Brown*), Juanita Quigley (*Malvolia Brown*), Butch Jenkins (*Donald Brown*), Reginald Owen (*Farmer Ede*), Terry Kilburn (*Ted*), Alec Craig (*Tim*), Eugene Loring (*Mr. Taski*), Norma Varden (*Miss Sims*), Arthur Shields (*Mr. Hallam*), Dennis Hoey (*Mr. Greenford*), Aubrey Mather (*Entry Official*), Frederic Worlock (*Stewart*), Arthur Treacher (*Man with Umbrella*), Harry Allen (*Van Driver*), Billy Bevan (*Constable*).

Elizabeth Taylor made her film debut as a ten-year-old in a Universal B picture called *There's* *One Born Every Minute*. The film made no impression, but a year later it resulted in her being tested for a small role in *Lassie Come Home*, and this time both the picture and the incredibly beautiful little girl made a very definite impression. MGM put her under contract and straightaway loaned her to Fox to play the pitiful child who dies after harsh treatment in the boarding school in *Jane Eyre*. Next came a bit in *The White Cliffs of Dover* and then a leading role in *National Velvet*, which launched her to stardom. Whether viewed in 1944 or today, the film is charming, and Elizabeth's beauty and persuasiveness are astonishing.

This is yet another of MGM's English pictures made in California, and it is especially notable for the lengthy sequence depicting the celebrated Grand National Steeplechase. This exciting and spectacular sequence runs ten minutes and involves some beautiful horses and splendid horsemanship, particularly that of Elizabeth Taylor, who, like the girl she was playing, loved horses. She spent many hours training herself for the role.

Mickey Rooney, Elizabeth Taylor and Anne Revere.

Reginald Owen, Elizabeth Taylor and Mickey Rooney.

Donald Crisp and Elizabeth Taylor.

Here she is a girl who wins a fractious horse in a raffle and dreams of entering it in the Grand National, encouraged by her understanding mother (Anne Revere) but cautioned by her conservative father (Donald Crisp). Her ally and trainer is a young, embittered drifter (Mickey Rooney) who is offered accommodation by her family and given a job by the father. He is a former jockey, down on his luck, who gains spiritual rehabilitation from this family and from his belief in the girl and her horse.

Director Clarence Brown had been at MGM since the early twenties, and by the time he made *National Velvet* he was the studio's top man, having made many of Garbo's pictures. He was a personification of MGM style, an expert at turning out glossy entertainment for a wide general audience, and this film is "company policy" at its very best. The content and construction of the picture are faultless, and in casting Elizabeth Taylor as young Velvet the studio could hardly have been luckier. Here, gorgeous and innocent, she barely seems related to the actress who would twenty-two years later appear as Martha in *Who's Afraid of Virginia Woolf?* and other shrieking harridans.

Rosalind Ivan and Charles Laughton.

The Suspect

Ella Raines and Charles Laughton.

1945

A Universal Production; produced by Islin Auster; directed by Robert Siodmak; screenplay by Bertram Millhauser, adapted by Arthur T. Hormen from a novel by James Ronald; photographed by Paul Ivano; musical score by Frank Skinner; running time, 85 minutes.

Cast: Charles Laughton (*Philip*), Ella Raines (*Mary*), Dean Harens (*John*), Stanley Ridges (*Huxley*), Henry Daniell (*Mr. Simmons*), Rosalind Ivan (*Cora*), Molly Lamont (*Mrs. Simmons*), Raymond Severn (*Merridew*), Eve Amber (*Sybil*), Maude Eburne (*Mrs. Packer*), Clifford Brooke (*Mr. Packer*).

Charles Laughton's film career in the forties was much less distinguished than in the thirties, when he had impressed critics with his portrayals of such figures as Henry VIII, Rembrandt, Captain Bligh, and Quasimodo. In the forties he settled for making a good living with parts in average comedies and dramas, the income from which allowed him to devote his remaining time to collecting *objets d'art,* performing and directing on the stage, and teaching a select group of drama students.

However, one film he made in this period deserves attention, not only for the actor's clever performance, but for the subtle direction given it by Robert Siodmak, who was a kind of German Hitchcock. Siodmak ran afoul of the Nazis in 1934 and made films in France until the German occupation, when he proceeded to Hollywood. His talent for suspense and the darker side of human nature showed up in such minor items as *Son of Dracula, Cobra Woman,* and *Phantom Lady,* and then Universal entrusted him with directing Deanna Dubin's first dramatic feature, *Christmas Holiday,* the success of which convinced Hollywood that here was a director with a distinct personal touch. *The Suspect* dispelled any lingering doubts.

The film is set in turn-of-the-century London and loosely based on the Crippen murder case. Laugh-ton plays a mild-mannered, pleasant shopkeeper whose life is blighted by a shrewish, nagging wife (Rosalind Ivan). He becomes acquainted with a nice young girl, Mary (Ella Raines), and when they fall in love he decides to kill the wife. He clubs her to death with a cane and successfully persuades the police that her injuries were caused in a fall downstairs.

Two men have their doubts—a detective (Stanley Ridges) and a vicious neighbor (Henry Daniell), who blackmails the shopkeeper. The neighbor becomes the next victim, and the detective quietly and doggedly persists until the shopkeeper confesses.

Siodmak considered *The Suspect* his best-told tale, and in telling it he had a major ally in Charles Laughton. The film has an atmosphere of subdued anxiety that comes from Laughton's compassionate portrayal of a basically decent man caught in fearful circumstances. The other main roles are also finely played—Ella Raines as a girl whose warmth might lead any middle-aged man astray, Rosalind Ivan as the dreadful virago, Stanley Ridges as the gentlemanly detective almost sorry to bring his quarry down, and the superlative Henry Daniell as the black-hearted neighbor.

Dean Harens, Eve Amber, Maude Eburne, Ella Raines, Clifford Brooke and Charles Laughton.

Charles Laughton and Stanley Ridges.

The Woman in the Window

1945

An International-Christie Production, released by RKO-Radio; produced by Nunnally Johnson; directed by Fritz Lang; screenplay by Nunnally Johnson, based on the novel *Once Off Guard*, by J. H. Wallis; photographed by Milton Krasner; musical score by Arthur Lange; running time, 99 minutes.

Cast: Edward G. Robinson (*Professor Richard Wanley*), Joan Bennett (*Alice Reed*), Raymond Massey (*District Attorney*), Dan Duryea (*Heidt*), Edmund Breon (*Doctor Blackstone*), Thomas E. Jackson (*Police Inspector Jackson*), Dorothy Peterson (*Mrs. Wanley*), Arthur Loft (*Mazzard*), Frank Dawson (*Steward*), Carol Cameron (*Elsie*), Bobby Blake (*Dickie*).

It might be said that Hollywood's most generous benefactor was Adolf Hitler. The Nazi regime forced numerous actors, composers, writers, photog-raphers, and directors to find their way to Califor-nia, giving the American film industry a strong and influential Germanic strain. The most successful of the directors were Otto Preminger, Billy Wilder, Robert Siodmak, and Fritz Lang.

Lang had made the famed *M* with Peter Lorre in 1931, and in 1936 he had disturbed Americans with *Fury*, an uncompromising treatment of mob vio-lence and injustice. His settling in Hollywood was uneasy and not very productive, but during the war he hit his stylistic stride with *Man Hunt*, *Hangmen Also Die*, and *Ministry of Fear*, each a thriller in a war setting.

Lang then turned away from war and made an intimate murder mystery, *Woman in the Window*, a chilling little tale, dark and somber and quite Germanic in its look and feel.

The woman of the title is actually a painting of a beautifully beguiling creature who causes Professor Richard Wanley (Edward G. Robinson), a lonely, introverted gentleman, to daydream and to yearn

Edward G. Robinson and Joan Bennett.

for her. He becomes involved with a sensuous young lady, Alice Reed (Joan Bennett), who looks much like the woman in the painting. She is much his social inferior, but he feels helplessly attracted to her. Visiting her in her apartment, Wanley is interrupted by a jealous suitor, who attacks him with a pair of scissors. In protecting himself, Wanley kills the man.

Fearing scandal, he decides to dispose of the body, which turns out to be a harrowing experience. The murdered man is a prominent financier, and Wanley's anxiety is increased when his good friend the district attorney (Raymond Massey) explains the intricate means by which he and the police intend to track down the murderer.

Wanley's plight is intensified when the financier's vicious bodyguard (Dan Duryea) moves to blackmail Wanley and Alice. It is all too much for the shattered professor, and he decides to kill himself. He sits in an armchair, drinks a glass of poison, and passes out.

The ending of *Woman in the Window* is something of a letdown. As Wanley sits unconscious in the chair, a hand moves to his shoulder and shakes him awake. The professor is in his club, and the whole bizarre story has been a bad dream. It is, however, not an unreasonable ending, and Lang's cunning direction and Robinson's highly plausible Wanley make this a classic example of film *noir*.

Dan Duryea and Joan Bennett.

Joan Bennett and Edward G. Robinson.

Stephen Bekassy, Merle Oberon and Cornel Wilde.

1945

A Columbia Production; produced by Louis F. Feldman; directed by Charles Vidor; screenplay by Sidney Buchman, based on a story by Ernst Marischka; photographed in Technicolor by Tony Gaudio; musical direction by M. W. Stoloff; running time, 113 minutes.

Cast: Paul Muni (*Professor Joseph Elsner*), Merle Oberon (*Georges Sand*), Cornel Wilde (*Fréderic Chopin*), Stephen Bekassy (*Franz Liszt*), Nina Foch (*Constantia*), George Coulouris (*Louis Pleyel*), Sig Arno (*Henri Dupont*), Howard Freeman (*Kalbrenner*), George MacCready (*Alfred deMusset*), Claire Dubrey (*Madame Mercier*), Frank Puglia (*M. Jollet*), Fern Emmett (*Madame Lambert*), Sybil Merritt (*Isabelle Chopin*), Ivan Triesault (*M. Chopin*), Fay Helm (*Madame Chopin*), Dawn Bender (*Isabelle as a child*), Maurice Tauzin (*Chopin as a child*).

A Song to Remember

For students of music, *A Song to Remember* is easy to criticize, since it greatly romanticizes the life of Fréderic Chopin and adds many fictional tissues. However, criticism on that level must be tempered with the understanding that in 1945 this film did a great deal to interest a wide public in Chopin's music. With the music adapted by Miklos Rozsa and performed by José Iturbi, there is much to enjoy and admire. Sales of Chopin recordings blossomed when this picture was shown, and presumably a great many people had their appetites for serious music whetted.

According to Sidney Buchman's screenplay, Chopin (1810–1849) was a political idealist who devoted much of his career to espousing the cause of his native Poland in its struggle to throw off czarist oppression. As a young man Chopin (Cornel Wilde) sides with the revolutionaries, to the concern of his sagacious teacher and mentor Joseph Elsner (Paul Muni). When Chopin goes to Paris to win fame and money to support his political friends, Elsner accompanies him, to guide and protect him.

In the halls of a music publisher Chopin makes the acquaintance of Franz Liszt (Stephen Bekassy), who is already an admirer of the young Pole's compositions. Liszt befriends him, promotes his career, and brings him into contact with the elegant and firmly feminist novelist Georges Sand (Merle Oberon). The tempestuous couple fall in love and Chopin, against Elsner's advice, goes with her to Majorca, where he becomes ill.

The lovers quarrel, and the now consumptive pianist-composer exhausts himself with a concert tour to raise money for his patriot friends. He dies, estranged from the woman he loves.

The facts are that Chopin was never a revolutionary and pursued a career without political motivation. He went to Paris alone, and his affair with Georges Sand spanned ten years. After they ended their relationship it was Chopin who refused her offers of reconciliation. However, Columbia Pictures can well point out that this is the only movie about the life of a serious composer to make a killing at the box office. It made a star of Cornel Wilde, who was actually too well built to be believable as the frail and petulant Chopin but gave an interesting and sincere performance. Wilde studied the piano for months to master the fingering and match the playing of Iturbi, and he did it so well that he afterward received several offers for concert tours.

Paul Muni and Cornel Wilde.

Cornel Wilde, Merle Oberon and Paul Muni.

Claire Trevor and Dick Powell.

Douglas Walton and Dick Powell.

Murder, My Sweet

1945

An RKO-Radio Production; produced by Adrian Scott; directed by Edward Dmytryk; screenplay by John Paxton, based on the novel *Farewell, My Lovely*, by Raymond Chandler; photographed by Harry J. Wild; musical score by Roy Webb; running time, 95 minutes.

Cast: Dick Powell (*Philip Marlowe*), Claire Trevor (*Mrs. Grayle*), Anne Shirley (*Ann Grayle*), Otto Kruger (*Amthor*), Mike Mazurki (*Moose Malloy*), Miles Mander (*Mr. Grayle*), Douglas Walton (*Marriott*), Don Douglas (*Lieutenant Randall*), Ralf Harolde (*Doctor Sonderberg*), Esther Howard (*Mrs. Florian*).

For Dick Powell *Murder My Sweet* was an important change of image in a sagging career. The picture's success enabled him to establish himself as an actor of considerable ability. All through the thirites Powell had appeared as a boyish crooner in Warner Bros. musicals, and after three dozen of

them he was desperate to break away from this narrow avenue.

He gave an indication of greater talent in Preston Sturges' modestly successful satire *Christmas in July* (1940), and in 1942 he accepted a Paramount contract in the belief that it would bring interesting opportunities. Instead, Paramount put him in a string of musicals—*Star Spangled Rhythm, Happy Go Lucky, True to Life*, and *Riding High*—and refused to give him the lead in *Double Indemnity*. Powell then asked for, and received, his release from Paramount.

He next did well by Rene Clair's comedy-fantasy *It Happened Tomorrow*, and when producer Adrian Scott decided to make a film of Raymond Chandler's *Farewell, My Lovely*, the central figure of which was a down-at-heel and not particularly scrupulous private detective named Philip Marlowe, he asked Powell if he would be interested in the role.

Movies about detectives had always been plentiful and popular, but *Murder My Sweet* brought a

Dick Powell, Miles Mander and Anne Shirley.

new concept to the genre. Here was realism and an uncompromising look at dark enterprises and sleazy characters. The story is set in Hollywood, but it shows the underside of the town, in marked contrast to its supposedly glamorous image.

Philip Marlowe operates from a grubby office and works for twenty-five dollars a day and expenses. He is hired by a huge, dim brute, Moose Malloy (Mike Mazurki), to find a missing girl, and in tracing her he runs afoul of several vicious, crooked people, including a lethal blonde (Claire Trevor) and a quack doctor (Otto Kruger). Marlowe finds himself in a complex situation revolving around a missing jade necklace, with attendant murders and double crosses. Before he has solved the case, Marlowe is brutally beaten, cheated, and drugged. But to him, it is all in a day's work.

Dick Powell was perfect as the glib, sardonic Marlowe. Long at ease in front of movie cameras, he had also developed an excellent speaking voice, which assured him a profitable secondary career in radio. Powell had sung on radio all through the years of his movie musicals, but with his new image he sang less and acted more. His radio series "Richard Diamond, Private Detective" was popular for several years before his switch to television in the early fifties.

An astute businessman, Powell was one of the

Anne Shirley and Dick Powell.

first movie stars to fully realize the impact of television and the opportunities it presented, and by the time of his death in 1963 he had become one of the television industry's most powerful executives.

In terms of his screen career, his most interesting period was the last half of the forties, which began with *Murder My Sweet* and continued with such well-produced and well-acted pictures as *Cornered, Johnny O'clock, To the Ends of the Earth, Pitfall, Stations West, Rogue's Regiment,* and *Mrs. Mike.*

141

Lowell Gilmore, Hurd Hatfield and George Sanders.

The Picture of Dorian Gray

1945

An MGM Production; produced by Pandro S. Berman; directed by Albert Lewin; screenplay by Albert Lewin, based on the novel by Oscar Wilde; photographed by Harry Stradling; musical score by Herbert Stothart; running time, 110 minutes.

Cast: George Sanders (*Lord Henry Wotton*), Hurd Hatfield (*Dorian Gray*), Donna Reed (*Gladys Hallward*), Angela Lansbury (*Sibyl Vane*), Peter Lawford (*David Stone*), Lowell Gilmore (*Basil Hallward*), Richard Fraser (*James Vane*), Douglas Walton (*Allen Campbell*), Morton Lowry (*Adrian Singleton*), Miles Mander (*Sir Robert Bentley*), Lydia Bilbrook (*Mrs. Vane*), Mary Forbes (*Lady Agatha*), Robert Greig (*Sir Thomas*), Moyna MacGill (*Duchess*), Billy Bevan (*Malvolio Jones Chairman*), Lillian Bond (*Kate*).

In the 1940s Hollywood produced many films *noir,* and perhaps the blackest, at least in the spiritual sense, was *The Picture of Dorian Gray.* This is not a totally successful visualization of Oscar Wilde's wickedly elegant novel—it is too glum and slow paced—but there is much to admire in scenarist-director Albert Lewin's handling of the bizarre material.

Lewin scored a casting coup by using Hurd Hatfield, a twenty-six-year-old stage actor, as Dorian Gray. Hatfield was a stranger to moviegoers, and his handsome, ethereal face and cool, aloof manners were perfect for Wilde's corrupted aristocrat.

To portray the acidly witty, cynical Lord Henry Wotton, disdainfully dropping epigrams, Lewin had to look no further than George Sanders. Lewin had previously used Sanders to great advantage in

142

Hurd Hatfield and George Sanders.

143

Hurd Hatfield and Angela Lansbury.

his excellent filming of Somerset Maugham's *The Moon and Sixpence* (1942), and the two worked together again in *The Private Affairs of Bel Ami* (1947). Sanders was a cad in them all—and no one played a cad more magnificently than he.

In Dorian Gray we are again in MGM's Victorian London, with ornate sets and foggy streets. Artist Basil Hallward (Lowell Gilmore) is fascinated by the youthful beauty and innocence of his friend Dorian Gray and captures it all in a masterly oil painting. Gray is then obsessed with the idea of retaining his beauty, and in wanting to live life to the fullest he is egged on by the amoral Lord Henry.

Gray stands before his portrait and vows that he will give up his soul if the likeness will take on all the appearances and penalities of age and experience, leaving him youthful. He gets his wish and indulges in a life of hedonism and cruel selfishness, while through the years his face is changeless. The portrait, however, grows vile and hideous.

When the artist discovers the secret, Gray kills him. He also causes the death of a demure young cabaret singer, Sybil Vane (Angela Lansbury), and when her brother catches up with him many years later, the brother gives up in confusion, believing that the youthful-looking Gray cannot be the culprit.

As time goes by Gray becomes weary and satiated with life, and in a moment of rage he takes a knife and stabs his portrait. As the knife rips the canvas, Gray falls dead. The portrait resumes its initial appearance, and the corpse takes on the decayed and repulsive age.

Harry Stradling's superbly shaded black-and-white photography gives this film a macabre atmosphere, and in its final scene the screen suddenly and shockingly bursts into Technicolor. Hurd Hatfield never progressed to stardom, but in Hollywood history he will always rightly be remembered as the man who played Dorian Gray.

144

Dean Stockwell, Gene Kelly, Kathryn Grayson and Frank Sinatra.

Anchors Aweigh

1945

An MGM Production; produced by Joe Pasternak; directed by George Sidney; screenplay by Isobel Lennart, based on a story by Natalie Marcin; photographed in Technicolor by Robert Planck and Charles Boyle; songs by Jule Styne and Sammy Cahn; musical direction by George Stoll; running time, 143 minutes.

Cast: Frank Sinatra (*Clarence Doolittle*), Kathryn Grayson (*Susan Abott*), Gene Kelly (*Joseph Brady*), José Iturbi (*himself*), Dean Stockwell (*Donald Martin*), Pamela Britton (*Brooklyn Girl*), Rags Ragland (*Police Sergeant*), Billy Gilbert (*Café Manager*), Henry O'Neill (*Admiral Hammond*), Carlos Ramirez (*Carlos*), Edgar Kennedy (*Police Captain*), Grady Sutton (*Bertram Kraler*), Leon Ames (*Admiral's Aide*), Sharon McManus (*Little Beggar Girl*).

MGM musicals of the forties have a particularly nostalgic appeal. This was a time when the studio was the biggest and richest of all the film factories.

Talent of all kinds was available in abundance, as was a huge audience, and on several occasions MGM packed its musicals with guest stars. The main plot device on these projects was the show within the show. Usually this would be a benefit staged in the interests of the armed forces or the picture would be set in Hollywood and the guest stars would appear as themselves.

Anchors Aweigh is one of the better entries in this field, thanks mostly to the engaging presence of Gene Kelly. This was also Frank Sinatra's first major screen appearance, at a time when the young crooner was a teenage idol.

Hollywood's wartime record is admirable. The town-industry opened its doors to all servicemen and spared no effort to entertain them. The hospitality was total, and not unnaturally it occurred to the studios to build a few films around this theme.

In *Anchors Aweigh* Kelly and Sinatra are sailors who decide to spend their shore leave in Hollywood. They meet girls with whom they fall in love. Kelly's girl is a movie extra and a singer in training, and through her he gets to visit MGM. Susan (Kathryn

Grayson) is a pupil of José Iturbi, who accompanies her as she sings "Jalousie" and later entertains with a little boogie-woogie and a bit of Tchaikovsky.

The songs of Jule Styne and Sammy Cahn provide Kelly and Sinatra with opportunities to dance and sing. The most charming song is Sinatra's "I Fall in Love Too Easily," and Kelly performs three major dance routines. He does "The Mexican Hat Dance" with a little girl and dances an elaborate fandango to the melody of "La Cumparsita." The highlight of the film is a dance-fantasy on a fairytale theme, "The King Who Couldn't Dance," in which Kelly dances with cartoon character Jerry the Mouse. The sequence is both clever and delightful.

Gene Kelly had pleased the public in several previous pictures, but *Anchors Aweigh* fully launched him as an entertainer of unique appeal, as well as winning him an Oscar nomination. In 1949 he and Sinatra appeared again as sailors on leave, in *On the Town,* a much more skillful film and an important breakthrough in screen choreography. However, *Anchors Aweigh* can be claimed as a more typical example of the superduper MGM musical of the forties.

Sharon MacManus and Gene Kelly.

Joan Crawford, Ann Blythe and Bruce Bennett.

Mildred Pierce

1945

A Warner Bros. Production; produced by Jerry Wald; directed by Michael Curtiz; screenplay by Ranald MacDougall, based on the novel by James M. Cain; photographed by Ernest Haller; musical score by Max Steiner; running time, 111 minutes.

Cast: Joan Crawford (*Mildred Pierce*), Jack Carson (*Wally Fay*), Zachary Scott (*Monte Beragon*), Eve Arden (*Ida*), Ann Blythe (*Veda*), Bruce Bennett (*Bert*), George Tobias (*Mr. Chris*), Lee Patrick (*Maggie Binderhof*), Moroni Olson (*Inspector Peterson*), Jo Anne Marlowe (*Kay Pierce*), Barbara Brown (*Mrs. Forrester*).

Mildred Pierce is a classic example of an actress finding just the right vehicle just in time. Joan Crawford had begun her screen career at the age of twenty-one in 1925, playing small parts in MGM pictures. She stayed with that studio for the next eighteen years, becoming one of its major stars, but she left in 1943, feeling that MGM no longer considered her popular enough to promote her with top features.

She then signed with Warner Bros. and did nothing for a year because they, too, failed to come up with sufficiently interesting projects.

The slump in her career came to an end with *Mildred Pierce*. As soon as she read the script she agreed to make the picture. Here, in her opinion, was something really worth doing—it was melodramatic, but it was literate, and it dealt with a woman of believable substance.

Mildred is an intelligent but discontented woman. Her husband (Bruce Bennett) is nice but ineffectual, and he drifts away to find solace with another woman when he realizes that neither his wife nor his two daughters care much about him.

The elder daughter, Veda (Ann Blythe), is spoiled by her mother, who takes menial jobs to give the girl good clothes and an education. Veda appreciates none of this.

With the help of a real estate man (Jack Carson), Mildred opens a small restaurant and makes the acquaintance of Monte Beragon (Zachary Scott), an elegant but financially embarrassed playboy. She persuades Monte to let her use one of his posh properties as a restaurant location. The

Zachary Scott, Jack Carson and Joan Crawford.

Zachary Scott, Ann Blythe and Joan Crawford.

business becomes greatly successful and develops into a chain of restaurants.

Mildred's problems increase with her affluence. She falls in love with Monte but changes her mind about him when she realizes that he is much more interested in her daughter than in her. However, she agrees to marry Monte if he will provide the high-society family background she feels will enable Veda to make good social contacts. In return Monte demands partnership in her business.

His profligate ways result in bankruptcy for the company, and Veda, who has been carrying on with him behind her mother's back, kills him when he finally rebuffs her.

Mildred takes the blame for the murder in order to save Veda, but the police soon arrive at the truth. She returns to her first husband, who is eager to have her back.

Joan Crawford won an Oscar for *Mildred Pierce*, and her admirable performance was backed by every highly professional department of Warner Bros., including a Max Steiner score, Ernest Haller photography, and the crisp, unsentimental direction of the remarkable Michael Curtiz.

150

Roughly Speaking

1945

A Warner Bros. Production; produced by Henry Blanke; directed by Michael Curtiz; screenplay by Louise Randall Pierson, based on her book; photographed by Joseph Walker; musical score by Max Steiner; running time, 117 minutes.

Cast: Rosalind Russell (*Louise Randall*), Jack Carson (*Harold Pierson*), Robert Hutton (*John*), Andrea King (*Barbara*), Donald Woods (*Rodney Crane*), Craig Stevens (*Jack Leslie*), Alan Hale (*Mr. Morton*), Ann Doran (*Alice Abbott*), John Alvin (*Lawton Mackail*), John Qualen (*Sven Olsen*), Ray Collins (*Mr. Randall*), Kathleen Lockhart (*Mrs. Randall*), Cora Sue Collins (*Elinor Randall*), Ann Todd (*Louise as a child*), Arthur Shields (*Minister*).

Michael Curtiz's next film for Warners, after *Mildred Pierce*, was also the saga of a courageous and enterprising woman, and it, too, was a vehicle for a former MGM star—Rosalind Russell. *Roughly Speaking* was released in October 1945, only a

month after the release of *Mildred Pierce*, which made the hardworking Curtiz seem even more prolific. Curtiz averaged two films a year throughout the forties, and each was a major production. The Joan Crawford picture was completed by the end of 1944, but Warners held it back for release at what they considered a propitious time. *Roughly Speaking* required a full four months of shooting, much longer than usual for a Warners film.

Indeed, the main fault of this one is its length. It tells the life story of Louise Randall Pierson, who wrote the screenplay, based on her autobiography. The film spans a forty-year period and is almost unavoidably episodic and long winded. However, many of the episodes are delightful, and the picture is a showcase for the talents of Rosalind Russell, one of the few Hollywood actresses able to temper a commanding presence with a comedic touch.

The story, which begins in 1902, waved the banner of feminism long before the women's-liberation movement. At the start it establishes twelve-year-old Louise Randall (Ann Todd) as a girl of drive and determination, bound to cut a path

Rosalind Russell and Donald Woods.

Jack Carson, John Alvin, Ann Doran, Craig Stevens and Rosalind Russell.

through life. When next seen she is a young woman (Russell) attending a business college, intent on a career. She meets and charms a Yale aristocrat (Donald Woods) and embarks on what is really an unsuitable marriage. She becomes the mother of five children, but her gusty, enterprising nature finally proves too much for her restrained husband, and he quits the marriage.

Louise meets her next husband at a fancy-dress party. Harold Pierson (Jack Carson) is an easygoing, good-natured fellow, willing to try anything to make a living. They are an ideal couple, and they bluster their way through years of near poverty, each taking whatever job comes her or his way. The story ends in the early years of the Second World War, after the Piersons have sent their sons away to the service.

Roughly Speaking is a sentimental journey, perhaps a little too much of a trip, but it has charm and humor as it relates the adventures of a lady of slightly eccentric character. Obviously, Louise Randall Pierson would not have needed the aid of the women's-liberation movement. And neither would Rosalind Russell.

Rosalind Russell and Jack Carson.

Jeanne Crain and Dana Andrews.

State Fair

1945

A 20th Century-Fox Production; produced by William Perlberg; directed by Walter Lang; screenplay by Oscar Hammerstein II, based on the novel by Phil Strong; photographed in Technicolor by Leon Shamroy; songs by Richard Rodgers and Oscar Hammerstein II; musical direction by Alfred Newman and Charles Henderson; running time, 100 minutes.

Cast: Jeanne Crain (*Margy Frake*), Dana Andrews (*Pat Gilbert*), Dick Haymes (*Wayne Frake*), Vivian Blaine (*Emily*), Charles Winninger (*Abel Frake*), Fay Bainter (*Melissa Frake*), Donald Meek (*Hippenstahl*), Frank McHugh (*McGee*), Percy Kilbride (*Miller*), Henry Morgan (*Barker*), Jane Nigh (*Eleanor*), William Marshall (*Marty*), Phil Brown (*Harry Ware*), Paul Burns (*Hank*), Tom Fadden (*Eph*), William Frambes (*Pappy*).

Phil Strong's novel *State Fair* was first filmed in 1933 as a vehicle for Will Rogers. A pleasant bit of folksy Americana, it made a natural transition to musical form a dozen years later. In asking Rodgers and Hammerstein to supply the songs, 20th Century-Fox could hardly have made a better or more logical choice. The celebrated Broadway team had written and produced two landmarks of musical Americana, *Oklahoma!* and *Carousel,* and Fox commissioned Hammerstein to write the entire screenplay.

The script and the songs lift this simple little story to a level of great warmth and appeal. As they had in the legitimate theater, Rodgers and Hammerstein deepened the concept of the movie musical by making the songs a part of the plot.

The story, set in Iowa in the summertime, relates the experiences of the Frakes, a farm family, as they visit the annual state fair. The father (Charles Winninger) wants to win a prize with his huge boar, and his wife (Fay Bainter) hopes to impress the judges with her mincemeat. Their two children, Margy (Jeanne Crain) and Wayne (Dick Haymes), are at the "awkward age" and not quite sure what they want, except that each has a strong yearning for attention from the opposite sex. In this respect

153

Dick Haymes, Fay Bainter, Jeanne Crain and Charles Winninger.

Fay Bainter, Jeanne Crain and Dana Andrews.

they, too, become winners. Wayne meets and falls in love with a dance-band singer (Vivian Blaine), and after she clears up complications in her life she is free to return his love. Margy finds a similar situation with a newspaper reporter (Dana Andrews), and by the end of the story all doubts have been lifted and all the prizes won by the proper parties.

State Fair has a genial atmosphere, and it glows with the wit and compassion of Oscar Hammerstein II. These qualities were sadly lacking when Fox remade the picture in 1961. The 1945 version wafts along on six songs: "Our State Fair" sets the bouyant mood of the occasion; "It Might As Well Be Spring" lyrically spells out Margy's vague discontent (Luanne Hogan dubbed the singing for Jeanne Crain); "That's for Me" states the feelings of Wayne and his girlfriend; "All I Owe Iowa" expresses the views of the people at the fair; "Isn't It Kinda Fun" clearly reveals how Wayne feels about being in love; and "It's a Grand Night for Singing" makes a perfect closing song for a group of people who have had a marvelous day at the fair.

State Fair is not for the cynical or the jaundiced.

Dick Haymes, Vivian Blaine and Henry Morgan.

154

The Lost Weekend

1945

A Paramount Production; produced by Charles Brackett; directed by Billy Wilder; screenplay by Charles Brackett and Billy Wilder, based on the novel by Charles R. Jackson; photographed by John F. Seitz; musical score by Miklos Rozsa; running time, 99 minutes.

Cast: Ray Milland (*Don Birnam*), Jane Wyman (*Helen St. James*), Howard da Silva (*Nat*), Philip Terry (*Wick Birnam*), Doris Dowling (*Gloria*), Frank Faylen (*Bim*), Mary Young (*Mrs. Deveridge*), Lillian Fontaine (*Mrs. St. James*), Anita Bolster (*Mrs. Foley*), Lewis L. Russell (*Charles St. James*), Helen Dickson (*Mrs. Frink*), David Clyde (*Dave*), Eddie Laughton (*Brophy*).

Prior to *The Lost Weekend,* drinking on the screen was primarily a subject for humor, but by the mid-forties Hollywood was daring to be more realistic in dealing with human faults and failings. There is nothing in the least comedic about the protagonist of *The Lost Weekend,* whose craving for alcohol leads him into nightmarish illness. Producer Charles Brackett and director Billy Wilder wrote the script and claimed that it was relatively easy, owing to the excellent construction of Charles R. Jackson's novel.

The decision to use Ray Milland as the star was bold, since the role was an abrupt departure from his image. The cultured Welshman (real name, Reginald Truscott-Jones) had made his Hollywood

Philip Terry, Jane Wyman and Ray Milland.

mark as a smooth, dapper leading man in light comedies, of which Wilder's *The Major and the Minor* (1942) was typical. Having worked with Milland, Wilder and Brackett knew that he was more capable than his previous pictures might have led people to believe, and they also realized that in casting Milland as a pitiful alcoholic they were increasing the film's impact.

Paramount was not in favor of making the film and hesitant to release it. To their surprise, it turned into a money maker. *The Lost Weekend* is not a pleasant picture, but it is totally fascinating in telling the story of a man's addiction to the bottle. Don Birnam (Milland) is a man of good background and a writer. Neither the care of his brother (Philip Terry) nor the understanding of his fiancée (Jane Wyman) is enough to ease his need for alcohol. He becomes increasingly devious and deceitful, and as his condition and his lack of cash worsen, he pilfers money, pawns his typewriter, and attempts to steal a girl's purse in a nightclub.

Alone in his room, Birnam sinks into delirium and imagines bats flying out of the walls. Later, in the alcoholic ward of New York's Bellevue hospital, he is subjected to the grim and chilling misery of psychiatric incarceration. Afterward, he pawns his girl's fur coat, so that he can buy a gun to commit suicide, but she manages to talk him out of it.

The movie ends on a note of hope—the only major variance from the Jackson novel.

The film won four major Oscars—as best film of 1945, to Milland as best actor, to Wilder as best director, and to Wilder and Brackett for best screenplay. Unfortunately for Milland, *The Lost Weekend* provided him with something of a hangover—for years he was the butt of drunk jokes, and he was frequently pestered by people wanting either to buy him drinks or to make fun of his supposed need for drink. What bothered Milland most were the pleas for help from real alcoholics.

158

Ray Milland and Howard da Silva.

Ray Milland and Jane Wyman.

Kitty

1945

A Paramount Production; produced by Karl Tunberg; directed by Mitchell Leisen; screenplay by Darrel Ware and Karl Tunberg, based on the novel by Rosamund Marshall; photographed by Daniel L. Fapp; musical score by Victor Young; running time, 103 minutes.

Cast: Paulette Goddard (*Kitty*), Ray Milland (*Sir Hugh Marcy*), Patric Knowles (*Brett Hardwood*), Reginald Owen (*Duke of Malmunster*), Cecil Kellaway (*Thomas Gainsborough*), Constance Collier (*Lady Susan Dowitt*), Dennis Hoey (*Jonathan Selby*), Sara Allgood (*Old Meg*), Eric Blore (*Dobson*), Gordon Richards (*Sir Joshua Reynolds*), Michael Dyne (*Prince of Wales*), Edgar Norton (*Earl of Campton*), Patricia Cameron (*Elaine Carlisle*), Percial Vivian (*Doctor Holt*), Mary Gordon (*Nanny*).

The guiding force behind *Kitty* was its director, Mitchell Leisen, who had begun his film career as a set designer. He was knowledgeable about art and architecture, and his films consequently had a great sense of pictorial style. Since the film centered around the eighteenth-century British painter Thomas Gainsborough, Leisen spent a lot of time on research. He was concerned about the film's reception in England and relieved when British historical groups praised him for his taste and accuracy. Leisen tried to borrow two great Gainsborough paintings, *Pinky* and *The Blue Boy*, from the nearby Huntington Library in Pasadena, but permission was denied, and he settled for having his artists copy them. Leisen acquired a room of genuine period furniture, and this he afterward donated to the Huntington Library.

Rosamund Marshall's novel is a cross between *Pygmalion* and *Forever Amber*. Set in London in 1759 it tells the story of a beautiful guttersnipe, Kitty (Paulette Goddard), who rises from cockney rags to the riches of a duchess.

She comes to the attention of Thomas Gainsborough, who is intrigued with her basic beauty and paints her portrait. A scheming, foppish impoverished nobleman, Sir Hugh Marcy (Ray Milland), becomes her patron, and after refining her speech and manners he arranges a marriage that he hopes will benefit both himself and Kitty. Her husband conveniently dies, leaving the way clear for the eager and elderly Duke of Malmunster (Reginald Denny). Kitty is pregnant by her first husband, but she allows the old duke to think the child is his, and at the birth his joy is so great that he exhausts himself and dies of a heart attack. Duchess Kitty is now free to marry the man she has loved all along, the cunning Marcy.

Leisen's *Kitty* is a visual delight, beautifully framed in Technicolor and certainly the most authentic of Hollywood's British costume pictures. Leisen's artistic taste and knowledge are apparent in the scenes showing the studios of Gainsborough and Sir Joshua Reynolds, as well as in the vivid impression of the sorrows of a debtor's prison.

The vivacious Goddard, seldom more than a competent actress, put extra effort into this part. She was tutored in her English accent by the distinguished Constance Collier, whose own performance as a tippling aristocrat is a major contribution to the film.

Constance Collier, Ray Milland and Paulette Goddard.

Cecil Kellaway, Ray Milland, Paulette Goddard and Patric Knowles.

Ray Milland, Constance Collier and Paulette Goddard.

The Spiral Staircase

1946

An RKO-Radio Production; produced by **Dore Schary**; directed by **Robert Siodmak**; screenplay by **Mel Dinelli**, based on the novel *Some Must Watch*, by **Ethel Lina White**; photographed by **Nicholas Musuraca**; musical score by **Roy Webb**; running time, 83 minutes.

Cast: Dorothy McGuire (*Helen Capel*), George Brent (*Professor Warren*), Ethel Barrymore (*Mrs. Warren*), Kent Smith (*Doctor Parry*), Rhonda Fleming (*Blanche*), Gordon Oliver (*Steve Warren*), Elsa Lanchester (*Mrs. Oates*), Sara Allgood (*Nurse Barker*), Rhys Williams (*Mr. Oates*), James Bell (*Constable*).

To play a mute lead in a film requires an enormous sense of presence from an actor, particularly if the story is a chiller and the keynote is fear. Under such conditions pantomime can easily become absurd. It is greatly to Dorothy McGuire's

credit that she performed such a role in *The Spiral Staircase* with touching and total conviction.

The screenplay was based on Ethel Lina White's novel *Some Must Watch,* which had already been adapted into a radio play for Helen Hayes. However, several major changes were made for the screen version—the contemporary English setting was changed to a New England location in the early years of this century, and the heroine's affliction was changed from being a cripple to being a psychosomatic mute. The producers felt that if the girl were unable to voice her apprehension, the film would be more frightening and the audience would feel a greater identification with her predicament.

Helen (McGuire) is a serving girl in an old mansion ruled over by a wealthy, bed-ridden matriarch, Mrs. Warren (Ethel Barrymore). One of Mrs. Warren's sons is a middle-aged professor (George Brent), and the other is the much younger Steve (Gordon Oliver).

Because of a shock as an infant, Helen has lost

the power of speech, but she is nevertheless a happy, sweet-natured girl. The tenor of her life is rudely altered when a killer begins to terrorize the community, and since his victims are all young ladies with physical afflictions. Helen has good reason to suppose that she is on the murderer's list.

The truth of her apprehension gradually becomes apparent as shadows and noises bother her as she moves around the house and gardens. Suspicion falls on every member of the household, but the villain turns out to be the seemingly compassionate Professor Warren.

The Spiral Staircase is the kind of suspense thriller that depends for its effectiveness on the skill of the people who made it. Robert Siodmak was the perfect director, with his talent for dark, macabre tales. Flickering lights, creaking doors, and sudden gusts of wind punctuate the activities in the sinister house. With such technical skill at hand, Siodmak needed actors capable of projecting doubt and dread. From Miss McGuire he drew a finely shaded performance, and in Ethel Barrymore he had a veteran who easily communicated the feelings of a cantankerous and frightened old lady. The film is plausible and intelligent and thus all the more disturbing.

Rhonda Fleming and Dorothy McGuire.

Kent Taylor, Rhys Williams and George Brent.

Ethel Barrymore and Dorothy McGuire.

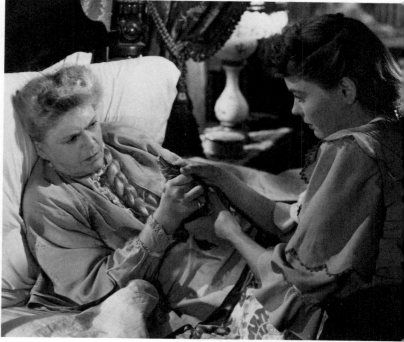

163

Cecil Kellaway, John Garfield and Lana Turner.

The Postman Always Rings Twice

1946

An MGM Production; produced by Carey Wilson; directed by Tay Garnett; screenplay by Harry Ruskin and Niven Busch, based on the novel by James M. Cain; photographed by Sidney Wagner; musical score by George Bassman; running time, 113 minutes.

Cast: Lana Turner (*Cora Smith*), John Garfield (*Frank Chambers*), Cecil Kellaway (*Nick Smith*), Hume Cronyn (*Arthur Keats*), Leon Ames (*Kyle Sackett*), Audrey Totter (*Madge Gorland*), Alan Reed (*Ezra Liam Kennedy*), Jeff York (*Blair*), Charles Williams (*Doctor*), Cameron Grant (*Willie*), Wally Cassell (*Ben*), William Halligan (*Judge*), Morris Ankrum (*Judge*), Garry Owen (*Truck Driver*).

Hollywood and James M. Cain did well by each other in the 1940s. Most novelists had reason to complain about the manner in which their material was adapted for movies, but the production values and intelligence put into *Double Indemnity*, *Mildred Pierce*, and *The Postman Always Rings Twice* must have pleased Cain. In each case the gritty reality of his rather nasty characters and their sleazy situations was translated into visual terms with genuine skill and credibility.

All these stories revolve around illicit love affairs, and all lead to murder. With *The Postman Always Rings Twice*, that is the entire substance of the plot. Tay Garnett's direction and the acting of John Garfield, Lana Turner, and the late Cecil Kellaway make it a coldly believable story.

Frank Chambers (Garfield) is a virile young man with no fixed address or occupation and few values. Making his way along a coastal road in California, he stops for a meal at a small service station–restaurant. The owner, a fiftyish, genial man named Nick Smith (Kellaway), senses that Frank is hard put to pay his bill and offers him a job as a handyman. The situation is complicated because Nick's wife, Cora (Turner), is very attractive and barely half her husband's age. Cora at first rebuffs Frank's advances but with time she inevitably gives in.

Nick is a happy, goodhearted man who fails to realize what is happening. A local district attorney (Leon Ames) senses a potentially explosive situation and keeps a watchful eye from a distance. The feelings Frank and Cora have for each other deepen, and even though they try to part, they can't.

They decide to kill Nick. They get him drunk and drive into the mountains at night, then bludgeon him and push his body down a hillside. What they assume to be a perfect crime falls apart when the district attorney discovers enough circumstantial evidence to incriminate them.

The lovers are divided and turned against each other through the machinations of a weasel of a lawyer (Hume Cronyn), and they are found guilty.

The plotline of *The Postman Always Rings Twice* is narrow and common, but its enactment here makes it harrowing and truly sad. John Garfield was excellent as the tough drifter and Lana Turner perfect as a young woman unable to save herself from a disastrous affair. But the acting of the greatly likable Cecil Kellaway, as the doomed Nick, gives the film its affecting poignancy.

John Garfield, Leon Ames and Lana Turner.

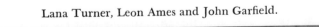

Lana Turner, Leon Ames and John Garfield.

166

To Each His Own

1946

A Paramount Production; produced by Charles Brackett; directed by Mitchell Leisen; screenplay by Charles Brackett and Jacques Thery; photographed by Daniel L. Fapp; musical score by Victor Young; running time, 100 minutes.

Cast: Olivia de Havilland (*Miss Norris*), John Lund (*Captain Cosgrove: Gregory*), Mary Anderson (*Corinne Piersen*), Roland Culver (*Lord Desham*), Philip Terry (*Alex Piersen*), Bill Goodwin (*Mac Tilton*), Virginia Welles (*Liz Lorimer*), Victoria Horne (*Daisy Gingras*), Griff Barnett (*Mr. Norris*), Alma Macrorie (*Belle Ingram*), Bill Ward (*Griggsy*), Frank Faylen (*Babe*).

John Lund and Olivia de Havilland.

The story of an unwed mother giving up her baby and yearning to have him back, *To Each His Own* was not a sure-fire attraction for 1946 audiences. It was more in line with the soap operas of the thirties, like *Madame X* and *Stella Dallas,* but this film was so deftly directed by Mitchell Leisen and so beautifully acted by Olivia de Havilland that it became a major success.

After reading the script, Miss de Havilland immediately agreed to make the film, sensing that it would give her wide opportunities, but she astutely requested her own choice of director. She had worked with Leisen in *Hold Back the Dawn* in 1941 and reasoned that *To Each His Own* needed his brand of taste and artistic maturity. At first Leisen declined, feeling that the story was trite and old-fashioned, but de Havilland and producer-writer Charles Brackett persuaded him to make the film.

The story begins in London during the Second World War, with a middle-aged American spinster, Josephine Norris (de Havilland), and Lord Desham (Roland Culver) on duty as air-raid wardens. They become friends, and Miss Norris confides in him.

She hears that a young American officer, Gregory Pierson (John Lund), has arrived in London, and her thoughts fly back to her hometown in 1917. She remembers how she met a handsome aviator, Captain Cosgrove (also Lund), and fell in love with him. Soon, expecting his child, she learned that he had been killed in action. She gave up the child for adoption, then quickly regretted the decision. Unable to reclaim the boy, she devoted her life to business and became successful in the cosmetics industry, which eventually brought her to London.

Finally she has the chance to see her grown son. She invites him to stay at her apartment but does not reveal her relationship to him. Lord Desham drops sufficient hints for Gregory to realize who she is, and the film ends in a nightclub with Gregory walking up to Miss Norris and saying, "Mother, I think this is our dance."

Olivia de Havilland had broken her contract with Warner Bros. to find better roles, and *To Each His Own* proved that she had known what she was doing. When she accepted the Oscar as best actress for this performance, she gracefully acknowledged the help of a fine script and the strong, skillful guidance of director Leisen.

Olivia de Havilland and John Lund.

Virginia Welles, John Lund, Olivia de Havilland and Roland Culver.

Anna and the King of Siam

1946

A 20th Century-Fox Production; produced by Louis D. Lighton; directed by John Cromwell; screenplay by Talbot Jennings and Sally Benson, based on the book by Margaret Landon; photographed by Arthur Miller; musical score by Bernard Herrmann; running time, 128 minutes.

Cast: Irene Dunne (*Anna*), Rex Harrison (*the King*), Linda Darnell (*Tuptin*), Lee J. Cobb (*Kralahome*), Gale Sondergaard (*Lady Thiang*), Mikhail Rasumny (*Alak*), Dennis Hoey (*Sir Edward*), Tito Renaldo (*Prince*), Richard Lyon (*Louis Owen*), William Edmunds (*Monshee*), John Abbott (*Phya Phrom*), Leonard Strog (*Interpreter*), Mickey Roth (*Prince*), Connie Leon (*Beebe*), Diana Van den Ecker (*Princess Fa-Ying*), Marjorie Eaton (*Miss McFarlane*), Addison Richards (*Captain Orton*).

The Rodgers and Hammerstein musical *The King and I* and the fine film version made in 1956 have unfortunately caused the nonmusical account to be shoved into obscurity. The musical, with Deborah Kerr and Yul Brynner, is difficult to criticize, but *Anna and the King of Siam* is less sentimental and closer to the drama and pathos of the original story. It also has superb production values, notably the musical scoring of Bernard Herrmann, who flavored the picture with suitably exotic tones, and the crystal-clear black-and-white photography of Arthur Miller, so well lit and shaded that it almost suggests color. And from Irene Dunne and Rex Harrison, the veteran John Cromwell drew performances of perfection. If *Anna and the King of Siam* is forever lost to film enthusiasts, it will be a sad blunder on the part of its owners.

Margaret Landon's book, a bestseller in the early

forties, related the actual adventures of an English-woman, Anna Leonowens (the name was shortened to Owens for the film), who went to Siam in 1862 and spent five years as secretary-tutor-confidante to King Mongkut.

Mrs. Leonowens was thirty-three when she returned to England. She became a journalist and lecturer, getting good mileage from her experiences dealing with the king, his huge harem, and his sixty-seven children.

She brought touches of culture, finesse, and leniency to Siam, as the king had hoped she would. The film shows the discomfort of Anna's initial tasks, her conflicts with the king, and the respect that grows between them, with never a hint of romance. Anna finds herself a teacher in a country where women are treated as a lower species—she befriends the gentle Lady Thiang (Gale Sondergaard), the first wife of the king, long relegated to the shadows, and she regards with horror the king's execution of his lovely young favorite, Tuptin (Linda Darnell), when he discovers her to be unfaithful.

Lady Thiang is the mother of Prince Chulalongkorn, and with her help Anna grooms him to succeed the king when he dies. When the prince finally takes the throne, he is better educated and more civilized than his father.

Irene Dunne cannot be faulted for this beautiful characterization, and in Rex Harrison, here making his first appearance in an American career after many years on the British screen, she had a subtle, expert counterplayer.

Irene Dunne and Rex Harrison.

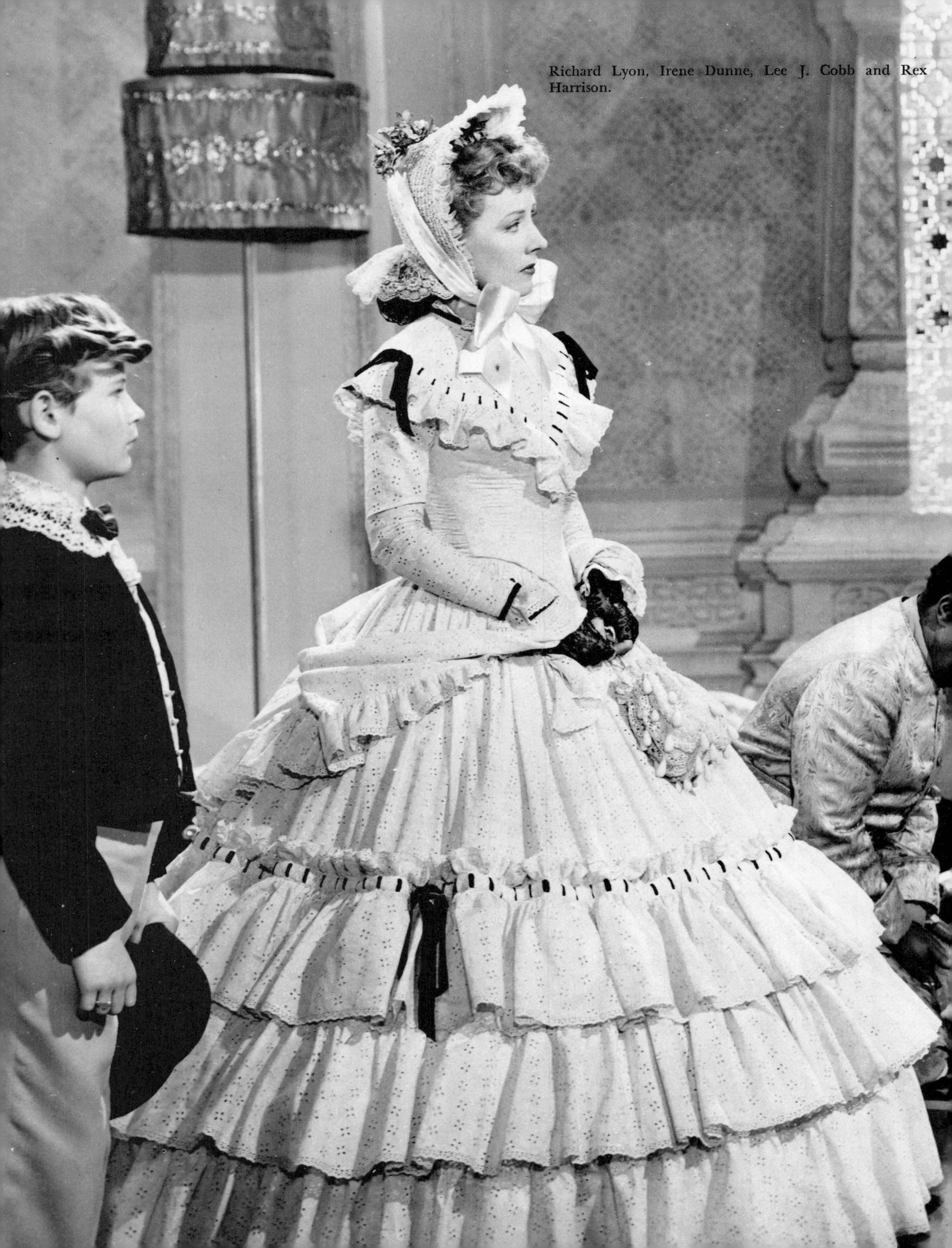

Richard Lyon, Irene Dunne, Lee J. Cobb and Rex Harrison.

Humphrey Bogart and Martha Vickers.

The Big Sleep

1946

A Warner Bros. Production; produced and directed by Howard Hawks; screenplay by William Faulkner, Leigh Brackett, and Jules Furthman, based on the novel by Raymond Chandler; photographed by Sid Hickox; musical score by Max Steiner; running time, 114 minutes.

Cast: Humphrey Bogart (*Philip Marlowe*), Lauren Bacall (*Vivian Rutledge*), John Ridgely (*Eddie Mars*), Martha Vickers (*Carmen Sternwood*), Dorothy Malone (*Bookshop Proprietress*), Peggy Knudsen (*Mrs. Mars*), Regis Toomey (*Bernie Ohls*), Charles Waldron (*General Sternwood*), Charles D. Brown (*Norris*), Bon Steele (*Canino*), Elisha Cook, Jr. (*Harry Jones*), Louis Jean Heydt (*Joe Brody*), Sonia Darrin (*Agnes*).

Humphrey Bogart worked at Warners throughout the thirties as a star of second magnitude, but in 1941 he really came into his own. That was the year of *High Sierra* and *The Maltese Falcon*. Then, with *Casablanca* in 1943, he became a major movie star and one of the top ten box-office winners for the remainder of the decade.

In 1945 Warners assigned an unknown twenty-one-year old actress to play opposite him in *To Have and Have Not*. Lauren Bacall was an instant success, with the public and with Bogart—he married her after completing the film. For their second picture Warners chose *The Big Sleep*, with Bogart playing Raymond Chandler's sardonic private eye, Philip Marlowe. The studio advertised it as "the picture they were born for," and aside from the hyperbole, it certainly was a suitable project for the stylish couple.

The plotlines of *The Big Sleep* are confusing. What is clear is that Chandler's title is a glib reference to death and that quite a few of the characters end up dead. Marlowe is hired by a wealthy, aged general to rid him of a blackmailer who threatens to circulate nude photos of his amatory daughter Carmen (Martha Vickers). The sensible older daughter, Vivian (Bacall), at first resents Marlowe but soon comes to his aid and then falls in love with him.

The incriminating photographs pass through various hands and cause murders all along the line. The principal villain is gambler Eddie Mars (John Ridgely), and when Marlowe has enough evidence he arranges a rendezvous with Mars. Mars tries to protect himself by having his gunmen surround the rendezvous, and Marlowe, after learning the truth, forces him out of the house at gunpoint and Mars is shot down by his own men. Marlowe and Vivian then wait for the police to arrive.

The Big Sleep is a triumph of style over material. Producer-director Howard Hawks gave it all the tight control and brisk pacing it needed, and the Bogart-Bacall pairing gave it their very individual flavoring. The picture is unmistakably a Warner Bros. product—its look, sound, and feel could be those of no other studio. One of the film's major assets is its score by Max Steiner. This was one of six pictures Steiner scored in 1946, but *The Big Sleep* clearly inspired him. The music punctuates the action as vividly as the gunshots and cleverly comments on the characters, particularly so with its jaunty theme for Marlowe and its rather earthy-romantic theme for him and his feisty girlfriend. Like the other elements of the film, the score is genuine film craftsmanship.

Charles D. Brown, Humphrey Bogart and Charles Waldron.

Lauren Bacall and Humphrey Bogart.

176

The Killers

1946

A Universal Production; produced by Mark Hellinger; directed by Robert Siodmak; screenplay by Anthony Veiller, based on a story by Ernest Hemingway; photographed by Woody Bredell; musical score by Miklos Rozsa; running time, 105 minutes.

Cast: Burt Lancaster (*Swede*), Ava Gardner (*Kitty Collins*), Edmond O'Brien (*Riordan*), Albert Dekker (*Colfax*), Sam Levene (*Lieutenant Lubinsky*), Jack Lambert (*Dum Dum*), Jeff Corey (*Blinky*), Donald McBride (*Kenyon*), Vince Barnett (*Charleston*), Charles D. Brown (*Packy*), Virginia Christine (*Lilly*), Phil Brown (*Nick Adams*), John Miljan (*Jake*), Charles McGraw and William Conrad (*the Killers*).

Burt Lancaster accepted a Paramount contract in 1945 on the strength of having made only one appearance in New York as an actor, in the play *The Sound of Hunting*. Before the war he had earned his living as a circus acrobat, but after serving in the army during the war he felt the need of something more intellectually challenging. He had the good fortune to be spotted by a producer and invited to audition, and he won the part with only one reading.

Even though *The Sound of Hunting* ran for only three weeks on Broadway, it brought Lancaster seven offers from Hollywood, and he took the Paramount contract because it allowed him to make one film a year for another studio. This worked out well for Paramount, because their first vehicle for Lancaster, *Desert Fury,* was not very impressive, and they held back on its release until 1947, when Lancaster had been seen in Universal's *The Killers.* With *The Killers,* Lancaster, whose physique and mystique made him a natural movie star, became an instant Hollywood fixture.

Anthony Veiller's screenplay is an imaginative expansion of a short story written by Ernest Hemingway in the twenties. It briefly tells of two gunmen waiting in a small diner for a man they have been hired to kill. The man is aware of them, and while they wait he lies in his dingy room, resigned to death and too world-weary to care what happens.

Jeff Corey, Burt Lancaster, Albert Dekker and Ava Gardner.

Charles McGraw, William Conrad and Harry Hayden.

Hemingway's story was an exercise in fatalism, and he gave no reason why the man had to die. Veiller wrote the Hemingway scenes into the beginning of the picture and then flashed back to what he imagined might have produced the situation.

In Veiller's view the man, Swede (Lancaster), is a boxer who has become involved in crime. Swede has allowed racketeers to take over his career, and through the cunning of a beautiful but deceitful girl (Ava Gardner) his life has become a mess. A powerful gangster (Albert Dekker) has used Swede for larcenous enterprises, and an insurance detective (Edmond O'Brien) has been assigned to unravel and solve the crimes. His investigations also explain why Swede meets his death in the manner set up by Hemingway.

Veiller's screenplay is complicated but absorbing, and skillfully directed by Robert Siodmak, who here furthered his reputation for setting up chilling suspense. Producer Mark Hellinger had originally wanted Wayne Morris to play Swede, but Warner Bros. wanted too high a price for his services, a circumstance that worked greatly in Hellinger's favor, since it caused him to use Lancaster. This is only one of many instances when profitable decisions have been made fortuitously. Hollywood history is full of them.

Ava Gardner and Burt Lancaster.

Larry Parks and William Demarest.

The Jolson Story

1946

A Columbia Production; produced by Sidney Skolsky; directed by Alfred E. Green; screenplay by Stephen Longstreet; photographed in Technicolor by Joseph Walker; musical direction by M. W. Stoloff; running time, 128 minutes.

Cast: Larry Parks (*Al Jolson*), Evelyn Keyes (*Julie Benson*), William Demarest (*Steve Martin*), Bill Goodwin (*Tom Baron*), Ludwig Donath (*Cantor Yoelson*), Tamara Shayne (*Mrs. Yoelson*), John Alexander (*Lew Dockstader*), Jo-Carroll Dennison (*Ann Murray*), Ernest Cossart (*Father McGee*), Scotty Beckett (*Jolson as a boy*), William Forrest (*Dick Glenn*), Ann E. Todd (*Ann as a girl*), Edwin Maxwell (*Oscar Hammerstein*), Emmett Vogan (*Jonsey*), Eddie Kane (*Ziegfeld*), and the voice of Al Jolson.

The Jolson Story was a gamble for Columbia Pictures. Several studios had tinkered with the idea of filming Al Jolson's life story, but the general feeling was that his name had little value in 1946 and that his style as an entertainer was passé. Jolson was now in his sixties, and his career had been lean for the past ten years. He had been the rave of Broadway in the twenties—modestly billed as "The World's Greatest Entertainer"—and he had starred in the first talkie, *The Jazz Singer* (1927).

In the first half of the thirties Warners starred him in a string of musicals, but his popularity quickly waned, and he returned to the stage. His departure from Hollywood was abetted by his lack of regard for the people for whom and with whom he worked. Jolson was a pathetically egocentric man who craved limelight and applause and showed little interest in anything else. However, Columbia's shrewd chieftain, Harry Cohn, had a hunch that the Jolson magic would still work.

The singer was too old to portray himself, even though he wanted to, and Larry Parks was cast as Jolson, with Jolson doing the singing and coaching Parks in his style and manner.

The film glossed over Jolson's actual story and left out the unpleasant parts, although it hinted that many of the ignored areas of his life had been caused by his driving force. It traced his early years as a vaudevillian, up through his many successes on Broadway and his importance in the first years of Hollywood talkies. But it played down his private life—here his main love was a girl called Julie Benson (Evelyn Keyes), but the part was based on Ruby Keeler, who refused to allow her name to be mentioned or to have anything to do with the picture. Of the many famous Jolson songs, "Sonny Boy" was conspicuously absent from the film. Jolson had virtually deserted and ignored Al, Jr.

Harry Cohn could hardly have been more astute in his hunch. *The Jolson Story* was a smash hit everywhere. A generation who had never heard of him went Jolson crazy—to his great delight. The belting baritone and the infectious singing style once more brought Jolson to the top of the entertainment world. Larry Parks, doing a masterly job of miming, was called upon two years later to do it all over again in a sequel, *Jolson Sings Again,* which proved almost as successful. In 1950 Jolson died, but he went out the way he wanted—loved and heralded by millions, leaving a legend in entertainment.

Larry Parks and Evelyn Keyes.

Bill Goodwin, Ludwig Donath, Tamara Shayne, Larry Parks, Evelyn Keyes and William Demarest.

My Darling Clementine

1946

A 20th Century-Fox Production; produced by Samuel G. Engel; directed by John Ford; screenplay by Samuel G. Engel and Winston Miller, based on a story by Sam Hellman and the book *Wyatt Earp, Frontier Marshal,* by Stuart Lake; photographed by Joseph MacDonald; musical score by Cyril Mockridge; running time, 97 minutes.

Cast: Henry Fonda (*Wyatt Earp*), Linda Darnell (*Chihuahua*), Victor Mature (*Doc Holliday*), Walter Brennan (*Pa Clanton*), Tim Holt (*Virgil Earp*), Cathy Downs (*Clementine Carter*), Ward Bond (*Morgan Earp*). Alan Mowbray (*Granville Thorndyke*), Don Garner (*James Earp*), John Ireland, Grant Withers, Mickey Simpson, Fred Libby (*the Clanton boys*).

John Ford's reputation as a master of the Western stems mainly from the second half of his career. He made many minor Westerns in his early days as a director, and his first major one was *The Iron Horse* in 1924. But fifteen years would pass before he made *Stagecoach,* the film that showed his true affinity for the genre, and another seven would pass before he made *My Darling Clementine.*

This exceptional Western brought back to the screen several actors who had been away in the war, among them Henry Fonda, Victor Mature, and Tim Holt. None could have asked for a better vehicle with which to resume his career, and for those among the critics and the public who thought the Western was passé, Ford demonstrated that all manner of subtle, complex dramatic and comedic material was possible in the setting of the old West. *My Darling Clementine* is so complex and subtle that it is open to any number of interpretations.

John Ford was a Catholic of strong moral precepts, and in many films he stated a firm belief in the value of family life. *My Darling Clementine* is a family picture, about a good family and a bad one —the Earps and the Clantons. The Earps settle in Tombstone, Arizona, when their youngest brother is killed in a cattle raid by outlaws. Wyatt (Henry Fonda) decides to take on the job of town marshal and in time uncovers evidence that the murderers are the Clantons, a renegade family whose father-leader (Walter Brennan) rules his four loutish sons with a whip.

Wyatt discovers that one of the most powerful men in town is a cynical, consumptive gambler known as Doc Holliday (Mature), and despite their disparate characters the two become friends. When Doc's Eastern fiancée, Clementine Carter (Cathy Downs), arrives in town he tries to send her away, claiming that both he and the life he leads are not for her.

Wyatt falls in love with Clementine but keeps his feelings to himself. His brother Virgil (Holt) meets his death at the hands of the Clantons, and when Doc's fiery girlfriend Chihuahua (Linda Darnell) dies as the result of Clanton antics, Doc joins with the Earps for direct action. The shootout at the OK Corral destroys the Clantons but also brings Holliday's life to an end.

My Darling Clementine is a dark, moody Western graphically photographed by the late remarkable Joseph MacDonald. It has the look and the atmosphere of the real wild West, all because of John Ford's persuasiveness.

This is fiction, and Ford never claimed otherwise. He shot the picture in Monument Valley, on the Utah-Arizona border, where the scenery is vastly different from the actual setting of Tombstone, in the southern part of the state. He was well aware that the facts about the Earp family and Doc Holliday are greatly different from those in his picture. Perhaps the best clue to Ford's attitude can be found in his *The Man Who Shot Liberty Valance* (1962), in which a newspaper editor says, "When the legend becomes fact, print the legend."

Linda Darnell and Henry Fonda.

Henry Fonda and Cathy Downs.

The Razor's Edge

1946

Tyrone Power, Herbert Marshall, Gene Tierney and John Payne.

A 20th Century-Fox Production; produced by Darryl F. Zanuck; directed by Edmund Goulding; screenplay by Lamar Trotti, based on the novel by W. Somerset Maugham; photographed by Arthur Miller; musical score by Alfred Newman; running time, 146 minutes.

Cast: Tyrone Power (*Larry Darrell*), Gene Tierney (*Isabel Bradley*), John Payne (*Gary Maturin*), Anne Baxter (*Sophie*), Clifton Webb (*Elliott Templeton*), Herbert Marshall (*Somerset Maugham*), Lucille Watson (*Mrs. Louise Bradley*), Frank Latimore (*Bob MacDonald*), Elsa Lanchester (*Miss Keith*), Fritz Kortner (*Kosti*), John Wengraf (*Joseph*), Cecil Humphreys (*Holy Man*), Harry Pilcer (*Specialty Dancer*), Cobina Wright, Sr. (*Princess Novemali*), Albert Petit (*Albert*), Noel Cravat (*Russian Singer*).

W. Somerset Maugham did well, at least financially, by Hollywood. His *Of Human Bondage* was filmed three times, *Rain* twice, *Vessel of Wrath* twice, and *The Letter* twice, in addition to a single version of *The Painted Veil*.

186

In the 1940 version of *The Letter,* the role of the sympathetic husband was played by Herbert Marshall, one of the most urbane of Hollywood's British gentlemen. When Maugham's *The Moon and Sixpence* was filmed in 1942 it happily occurred to someone to cast Marshall in the role of the Maugham-like author-narrator. He was an ideal choice, and four years later he was called upon to play Maugham in *The Razor's Edge.*

This is the most expensive filming of a Maugham story, and the author's admirers feel that it is one of the least authentic. Be that as it may, the film offers a great deal of entertainment, thanks to the intelligent script by Lamar Trotti, the tasteful decor of a team of set designers and art directors, the guidance of the cultured Edmond Goulding, some fine performances, and two of Fox's unfailingly fine ingredients—Arthur Miller photography and Alfred Newman music.

The story is long and complex. It concerns an idealistic young man, Larry Darrell (Tyrone Power), who returns from the First World War questioning his values and hoping to find sources of wisdom. He loves a society girl, the spoiled Isabel

Tyrone Power and Anne Baxter.

Gene Tierney, Clifton Webb, Herbert Marshall, Anne Baxter, John Payne and Tyrone Power.

(Gene Tierney), but she marries the rich Gary Maturin (John Payne).

Darrell spends several years in India and then goes to Paris, where Isabel and her husband now live with her elegant, snobbish uncle Elliott Templeton (Clifton Webb).

A mutual friend, Sophie, has become an alcoholic because she lost her husband and children in an auto accident, and more in pity than in love Darrell offers to marry her. The jealous Isabel contrives to break up the engagement by encouraging Sophie to drink. Sophie disappears and is later found to have killed herself.

Isabel is now willing to leave her husband for Darrell, but he is aware of what she has done, and he turns his back on her. He continues his travels in search of understanding and knowledge.

This was the film that brought Tyrone Power back to the screen after his years in the service, and it proved that he had greater ability than his prewar pictures had suggested. But the acting honors go to Clifton Webb for his prissy aristocrat and to Anne Baxter, who won an Oscar for her tragic Sophie.

Wyrley Birch.

Boomerang

Dana Andrews and Arthur Kennedy.

188

1947

A 20th Century-Fox Production; produced by Louis de Rochemont; directed by Elia Kazan; screenplay by Richard Murphy, based on the article "The Perfect Case," by Anthony Abbott; photographed by Norbert Brodine; musical score by David Buttolph; running time, 88 minutes.

Cast: Dana Andrews (*Harry L. Harvey*), Jane Wyatt (*Madge Harvey*), Lee J. Cobb (*Chief Robinson*), Arthur Kennedy (*John Waldron*), Sam Levene (*Dave Woods*), Robert Keith (*Mac McCreery*), Taylor Holmes (*T. M. Wade*), Ed Begley (*Paul Harris*), Karl Malden (*Lieutenant White*), Cara Williams (*Irene Nelson*), Lester Lonnigan (*Carey*), Barry Kelley (*Sergeant Dugan*), Lewis Leverett (*Whitney*), Wyrley Birch (*the Reverend George A. Lambert*).

One of the most important producers in Hollywood's postwar years was Louis de Rochemont, who had devised *The March of Time* in 1934 and gained a brilliant reputation for his concepts in newsreels and documentaries. He moved into feature-film production with *The House on 92nd Street* in 1946 and *13 Rue Madeleine* a year later. Both pictures dealt with espionage and used actual locations, and told their stories in the documentary style de Rochemont had pioneered in *The March of Time*.

His next film was *Boomerang*, which was shot in its entirety in Stamford, Connecticut, and Elia Kazan agreed to direct it because he, too, believed that the time had come for Hollywood to move out of its studios and bring greater reality to American films.

Boomerang is based on a true story, the unsolved murder of a priest in Bridgeport, Connecticut, in 1924. Bridgeport objected to the film's being made there, fearing that it might rake up unpleasant memories and bring them adverse publicity, and de Rochemont settled on Stamford because it seemed to him both typical of a small New England town and sufficiently picturesque. The town gladly cooperated, and many local people appear in small parts and as extras.

The central character of *Boomerang* is a state's attorney named Harry L. Harvey (Dana Andrews) —the role was inspired by the man who handled the real case, former U.S. Attorney General Homer Cummings—who is called to defend a vagrant, John Waldron (Arthur Kennedy), accused of killing an elderly, much-respected churchman. The evidence against Waldron seems conclusive. Eyewitnesses agree that his appearance fits their recollections of the man they saw leaving the crime, and after two days of police grilling the luckless, sick-of-life Waldron confesses.

Harvey does not believe the man is guilty, and being politically ambitious, he stakes his career on proving Waldron innocent. In doing this Harvey swims against the tide of police, public, and press eagerness to conclude the case. However, he does dig out the evidence that clears Waldron, although neither he nor anyone else ever finds the real culprit.

Boomerang's success brought new concepts to American filmmaking particularly in regard to location shooting. It began a new wave of reality in movies and allowed directors like Elia Kazan to tell their stories with much greater credibility.

Jane Wyatt and Dana Andrews.

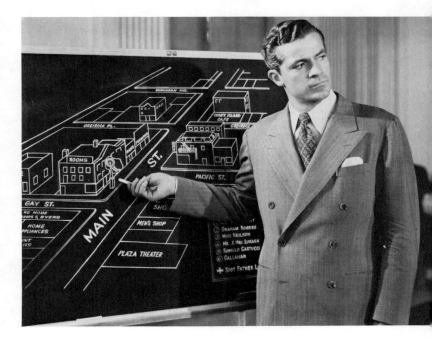

189

Charles Bickford, Ethel Barrymore and Loretta Young.

The Farmer's Daughter

1947

An RKO-Radio Production; produced by Dore Schary; directed by H. C. Potter; screenplay by Allen Rivkin and Laura Kerr, based on the play by Juhni Tervataa; photographed by Milton Krasner; musical score by Leigh Harline; running time, 97 minutes.

Cast: Loretta Young (*Katrin*), Joseph Cotten (*Glenn Morley*), Ethel Barrymore (*Mrs. Morley*), Charles Bickford (*Clancy*), Rose Hobart (*Virginia*), Rhys Williams (*Adolphe*), Harry Davenport (*Doctor Mathew Sutven*), Tom Powers (*Nordick*), William Harrigan (*Ward Hughes*), Lex Barker (*Olaf*), Don Beddoe (*Einar*), Anna Q. Nillsson (*Mrs. Holstrom*), Thurston Hall (*Wilbert Johnson*), Keith Andes (*Sven*), Harry Shannon (*Mr. Holstrom*), James Arness (*Peter*).

Joseph Cotten, Loretta Young, Charles Bickford and Ethel Barrymore.

The Oscar Loretta Young won for playing a working girl of Scandinavian origin in *The Farmer's Daughter* was well deserved, but it could also have served as recognition for her long and interesting career on the screen. Miss Young first appeared on film in 1927, when she was fourteen, and during the next twenty-six years she worked in no fewer than ninety pictures. Then, declaring her film career ended, she turned to television and with uncommon stamina and love for work spent eight years hosting her own dramatic series, appearing in half the programs as an actress. Her performances on "The Loretta Young Show" brought her three Emmy awards.

The farmer's daughter of the title is a bright, enterprising young lady named Katrin who sets out to become a nurse and makes her way to Capital City. En route she is swindled of her savings, and badly in need of work she takes a position as a maid in the home of a wealthy congressman, Glenn Morley (Joseph Cotten), and his matriarchal mother (Ethel Barrymore).

It soon becomes apparent to her employers and their outspoken butler (Charles Bickford) that Katrin is a woman of wide abilities and courage. No task is beyond her range. She cooks superbly, instructs Morley in skating, and even proves to be an excellent masseuse.

Morley grows ever more appreciative, and when he takes her to a political rally he watches in amazement as she speaks up and challenges the pronouncements of the candidates. Katrin's political savvy causes her to be swept into active duty—but not for Morley's party. When his side attempts to smear her reputation, Morley comes to her defense, and Katrin ends up not only winning a place in Congress, but also winning Morley as her husband.

This very pleasing comedy poked good fun at politics, especially in its rally scenes, with candidates mouthing elaborate, nonsensical dialogue. But the true winner in this film is Loretta Young, and when she was presented with her Oscar she understandably said, "At long last!" On an occasion some

years later when she was complimented on her remarkable career, the ladylike Loretta replied, "If
there's any difference between me and any other
woman my age, it's just that I've worked harder and
longer and with more concentration."

Rose Hobart, Joseph Cotten and Loretta Young.

Gregory Peck and Jennifer Jones.

Duel in the Sun

1946

A Vanguard Production, released by Selznick Organization; produced by David O. Selznick; directed by King Vidor; screenplay by David O. Selznick, adapted by Oliver H. P. Garrett from the novel by Niven Busch; photographed in Technicolor by Lee Garmes, Hal Rossen, and Ray Rennahan; musical score by Dimitri Tiomkin; running time, 138 minutes.

Cast: Jennifer Jones (*Pearl Chavez*), Joseph Cotten (*Jesse McCanles*), Gregory Peck (*Lewt McCanles*), Lionel Barrymore (*Senator McCanles*), Lillian Gish (*Laura Belle McCanles*), Walter Huston (*the Sinkiller*), Herbert Marshall (*Scott Chavez*), Charles Bickford (*Sam Pierce*), Joan Tetzel (*Helen Langford*), Harry Carey (*Lem Smoot*), Otto Kruger (*Mr. Langford*), Sidney Blackmer (*the Lover*), Tilly Losch (*Mrs. Chavez*), Scott MacKay (*Sid*), Butterfly McQueen (*Vashti*), Francis McDonald (*Gambler*), Victor Kilian (*Gambler*), Griff Barnett (*the Jailer*), Frank Cordell (*Ken*), Dan White (*Ed*), Steve Dunhill (*Jake*).

David O. Selznick hoped that *Duel in the Sun* would become a Western equivalent of *Gone with the Wind*. To that end he spent an enormous amount of time, effort, and money, but nothing he or his workers could do could make this gargantuan horse opera anything more than a very large slice of super *kitsch*. Selznick, who unwisely decided to write the screenplay himself, spent six million dollars on the trouble-beset project and then raised another two million to promote it.

The critics hacked away at it with delight, but the public flocked to see *Duel in the Sun,* whose sexy scenes soon won it the jargon title of *Lust in the Dust.* What defeats the film is the pretentious Wagnerian approach to what is really an operetta tale. What saves it are the skills of its technicians, especially the color photography of vast Western landscapes and some magnificently staged action sequences.

The two principal characters are Lewt McCanles (Gregory Peck) and Pearl Chavez (Jennifer Jones), he the raffish, spoiled son of cattle baron

194

Harry Carey, Joan Tetzel, Walter Huston, Joseph Cotten, Jennifer Jones, Gregory Peck,
Lionel Barrymore, Lillian Gish and Charles Bickford.

Senator McCanles (Lionel Barrymore) and she an
innocent half-breed who is sent to the McCanles
Ranch when her gambler father (Herbert Marshall) is hanged for killing his Indian wife and her
lover. Years before her father had been engaged to
Laura Belle (Lillian Gish), the senator's wife, and
he is sure she will take care of his daughter.

The older McCanles son, Jess (Joseph Cotten),
is a gentleman and Lewt is anything but. He
seduces Pearl but refuses to follow through on his
offer of marriage. Pearl then accepts the proposal of
ranch foreman Sam Pierce (Charles Bickford), but
the jealous Lewt goads him into a fight and kills
him.

The outlawed Lewt takes to the mountains to
hide out, but Pearl tracks him down. The two shoot
and mortally wound each other, but in their final
moments they realize their need for each other and
die in a bloody embrace.

Peck and Jones, backed by a suitably loud and
lush score by Dimitri Tiomkin, struggled admirably
to make sense of their rather ludicrous roles. More

Lionel Barrymore, Walter Huston and Lillian Gish.

Jennifer Jones and **Gregory Peck.**

convincing was the subplot dealing with the cattle baron's fight to stop the railroad from crossing his empire, resulting in splendid shots of hordes of horsemen riding furiously to a battle that never comes. As a regiment of cavalry draws up between the cowboys and the railroaders, Senator McCanles backs down—but he has no regrets when his dissolute son single-handedly wrecks an entire train. As Lewt rides away from the scene he quietly sings to himself, "I've been working on the railroad."

196

Gene Tierney and Robert Coote.

The Ghost and Mrs. Muir

1947

A 20th Century-Fox Production; produced by Fred Kohlmar; directed by Joseph L. Mankiewicz; screenplay by Philip Dunne, based on the novel by R. A. Dick; photographed by Charles Lang; musical score by Bernard Herrmann; running time, 104 minutes.

Cast: Gene Tierney (*Lucy*), Rex Harrison (*the Ghost of Captain Daniel Gregg*), George Sanders (*Miles Fairley*), Edna Best (*Martha*), Vanessa Brown (*Anna*), Anna Lee (*Mrs. Fairley*), Robert Coote (*Coombe*), Natalie Wood (*Anna as a child*), Isobel Elsom (*Angelica*), Victoria Horne (*Eva*), Whitfield Kane (*Sproule*), Brad Slaven (*Enquiries*), William Stelling (*Bill*), Helen Freeman (*Author*), David Thursby (*Sproggins*).

The Ghost and Mrs. Muir is the least frightening ghost story ever filmed. It is really a piece of romantic make-believe, but in the hands of director Joseph L. Mankiewicz the incredible becomes plausible. This is a graceful and warmly humorous movie about the relationship between a young widow and the spirit of a deceased sea captain in turn-of-the-century England.

Lucy (Gene Tierney) and her young daughter take up residence in an old house on the coast following the death of her husband in London. Lucy, whose air of independence shocks her genteel relatives, rents the house in spite of warnings that it is haunted. She soon has reason to believe the warnings, but rather than be intimidated by the supernatural, she calls upon the spirit to show himself. He reveals himself to be the handsome, bearded Captain Daniel Gregg (Rex Harrison), and it becomes apparent that he is more in favor of her presence than against it.

The two become friends, and when Lucy's money runs out Gregg, who doesn't want her to have to leave, suggests that he dictate his memoirs to her. These salty adventures find immediate acceptance with a London publisher, who expresses surprise that a woman could have written such virile tales.

In the publisher's office Lucy meets a gentlemanly author, Miles Fairley (George Sanders), who pays her court and soon leads her to believe that he will ask her to marry him. But Fairley turns out to be a

Gene Tierney and Rex Harrison.

George Sanders and Gene Tierney.

romantic fraud, as Lucy discovers when she meets his gentle, understanding wife (Anna Lee).

The sympathetic Gregg has come to love Lucy, but he realizes that he can bring her no real happiness, and he decides to take his leave. He speaks to Lucy as she sleeps and asks her to believe that he has existed only in her dreams.

The expertise of its players and its makers gives this picture its beautiful persuasiveness. In lesser hands it could be absurd, but with a director like Mankiewicz, a script by the literate Philip Dunne, a lovely and subtle musical score by Bernard Herrmann, and the artistry of Charles Lang's photography (he was nominated for an Oscar for this film), the whole thing has a pleasantly magical air. Rex Harrison, in his second American picture, is perfect as the ghost who hides his warmheartedness under a slightly cantankerous manner, and the elegant Gene Tierney, too often cast as a cold beauty, here glows with feminine appeal.

Maureen O'Hara, John Payne and Edmund Gwenn.

The Miracle on 34th Street

1947

A 20th Century-Fox Production; produced by William Perlberg; directed and written by George Seaton, based on a story by Valentine Davies; photographed by Charles Clarke and Lloyd Ahern; musical score by Cyril Mockridge; running time, 96 minutes.

Cast: Edmund Gwenn (*Kris Kringle*), Maureen O'Hara (*Doris Walker*), John Payne (*Fred Gailey*), Gene Lockhart (*Judge Henry X. Harper*), Natalie Wood (*Susan*), Porter Hall (*Mr. Sawyer*), William Frawley (*Politician*), Jerome Cowan (*District Attorney*), Philip Tonge (*Shellhammer*), James Seay (*Doctor Pierce*), Harry Antrim (*Mr. Macy*), Thelma Ritter, Mary Field (*Mothers*).

Christmas has been dealt with many times in the movies but never more pleasingly than in *The Miracle on 34th Street*. The idea for the story, having Santa Claus turn up at Macy's department store in New York and spread the spirit of the Yuletide in the very vortex of commercialism, came to George Seaton and Valentine Davies during a conversation on the treatment of Christmas on the screen. Together they completed a screenplay, and Seaton asked Darryl F. Zanuck to let him film it. Zanuck was not much impressed, but he agreed to a modest budget provided Seaton would accept his next assignment unconditionally.

Much of the film was shot in New York around Christmas of 1946, and Seaton secured the cooperation of Macy's. The studio, not impressed enough to hold back release until the following Christmas, sent the film out in June 1947.

Despite its untimely release, the movie caught the public fancy and in time gained the reputation of a fantasy classic.

The tale begins at the annual Christmas parade in New York when an advertising executive, Doris Walker (Maureen O'Hara), has to quickly find a substitute for the drunk she has hired to play Santa Claus. On hand is a genial, bearded gentleman (Edmund Gwenn) who readily accepts the job. She then hires him and pays little heed to his calling himself Kris Kringle.

Maureen O'Hara and John Payne.

Maureen O'Hara, Natalie Wood and John Payne.

Natalie Wood and Edmund Gwenn.

He delights children and parents with his cheery manner, but he dismays his employers when he sends customers to other stores to find the merchandise they cannot find at Macy's. His frankness in criticizing certain executives for their money-grubbing ways and his constant claim that he is actually Santa Claus lead to his arrest.

A young lawyer, Fred Gailey (John Payne), eagerly agrees to act as his lawyer, partly because he wants to romance Doris. Mr. Kringle is put on trial to determine his sanity. The perplexed judge (Gene Lockhart) is at a loss to prove whether there

is a Santa Claus, but when Fred brings in mailmen carrying endless sacks of letters addressed to Santa, the judge gives in. So does Doris, to the delight of her little girl (Natalie Wood).

George Seaton directed his material with just the right balance between reality and fantasy, but the real glory of the picture came from the performance of the veteran English actor Edmund Gwenn (1875-1959). His warm and winning portrait of Santa Claus remains one of the most appealing images in film history. That it won him an Oscar seems barely sufficient.

William Powell, Martin Milner and Irene Dunne.

Life With Father

1947

A Warner Bros. Production; produced by Robert Buckner; directed by Michael Curtiz; screenplay by Donald Ogden Stewart, based on the play by Howard Lindsay and Russell Crouse; photographed in Technicolor by Peverell Marley and William V. Skall; musical score by Max Steiner; running time, 118 minutes.

Cast: William Powell *(Father Clarence)*, Irene Dunne *(Vinnie)*, Elizabeth Taylor *(Mary)*, Edmund Gwenn *(the Reverend Doctor Lloyd)*, ZaSu Pitts *(Cora)*, Jimmy Lydon *(Clarence)*, Emma Dunn *(Margaret)*, Moroni Olsen *(Doctor Humphries)*, Elizabeth Risdon *(Mrs. Whitehead)*, Derek Scott *(Harlan)*, Johnny Calkins *(Whitney)*, Martin Milner *(John)*, Heather Wilde *(Anne)*, Monte Blue *(Policeman)*, Mary Field *(Nora)*, Queenie Leonard *(Maggie)*, Nancy Evans *(Delia)*, Clara Blandick *(Miss Wiggins)*, Frank Elliott *(Doctor Somers)*.

Clarence Day was an affluent New Yorker of commanding disposition who flourished in the late nineteenth century and ran his Madison Avenue home in an unyieldingly authoritarian manner. He would have vanished in the mists of time but for his son, Clarence Day, Jr., who captured his father's character and antics in a book of sketches called *Life with Father*.

In 1939 Howard Lindsay and Russell Crouse adapted the material into a play, and in that form it ran on Broadway for a solid eight years. That it should be made into a film was inevitable. Warner Bros. acquired the rights and hired the esteemed Donald Ogden Stewart to write a screenplay that would be faithful to the original but allow for the necessary expansion in terms of movement and the intimacy of the camera. The result satisfied all concerned, and the picture received the most deft performance imaginable from William Powell.

The title fully conveys the message; the film has

Irene Dunne and William Powell.

Irene Dunne and William Powell.

little plot. Clarence Day puts his finger on the crux of the story when, in response to an employment agency manager's inquiry about the character of his home, he proudly replies, *"I am the character of my home."* When he says this, he is in the process of hiring a maid, pointing with his cane and saying, "I'll take that one."

Maids pass through the Day home fairly swiftly, but his wife (Irene Dunne) and his three sons have learned to take their family head in stride. Mr. Day is constantly alarmed at his wife's failure to understand financial affairs, and in explaining the facts of life to young Clarence (Jimmy Lydon) he declares, "A woman doesn't think. She gets all stirred up." Then, after the briefest elaboration on that theme, he dismisses the boy with, "Now you know all about women."

However, when his wife becomes ill the seemingly agnostic Mr. Day commands God to have mercy. And because his wife has begged him for years to become baptized he promises God he will go to the font if she recovers. Her recovery is amazingly swift, and in the last scene of the film, as the family is on the way to church, a friend asks where they're going. He barks, "I'm going to be baptized, dammit!"

Life with Father is a delightful cameo of a bygone way of life, made impressive by William Powell's performance. It was only one of the twenty-one films of all kinds Michael Curtiz directed in the 1940s. Curtiz's range was prodigious, and his contribution to Hollywood history in this decade deserves great credit.

Elizabeth Taylor, William Powell and ZaSu Pitts.

Danny Kaye and Virginia Mayo.

The Secret Life of Walter Mitty

1947

An RKO-Radio Production; produced by Samuel Goldwyn; directed by Norman Z. Leonard; screenplay by Ken Englund and Everett Freeman, based on a story by James Thurber; photographed in Technicolor by Lee Garmes; musical score by David Raksin; songs by Sylvia Fine; running time, 105 minutes.

Cast: Danny Kaye (*Walter Mitty*), Virginia Mayo (*Rosalind Van Hoorn*), Boris Karloff (*Doctor Hugo Hollingshead*), Fay Bainter (*Mrs. Mitty*), Ann Rutherford (*Gertrude Griswold*), Thurston Hall (*Bruce Pierce*), Gordon Jones (*Tubby Wadsworth*), Florence Bates (*Mrs. Griswold*), Konstantin Shayne (*Peter Van Hoorn*), Reginald Denny (*RAF Officer*), Henry Gordon (*Hendrick*), Doris Lloyd (*Mrs. Follinsbee*), Fritz Feld (*Anatole*), Frank Reicher (*Maasdam*), Milton Parsons (*Butler*).

Danny Kaye bided his time about accepting offers from Hollywood during the years when he was making a name for himself on Broadway. In 1943 he signed a five-picture deal with Samuel Goldwyn, and the following year he launched himself into top stardom with *Up in Arms*. Kaye enjoyed a decade of popularity, and then his film career went into decline. Of his sixteen movies the most fondly remembered is *The Secret Life of Walter Mitty*, not because it was a great comedy but because it offered Kaye the most generous showcase for his unique talents.

Many admirers of James Thurber's short story were aghast at the manner in which it was pumped up into a huge picture, but the subject of Walter Mitty is so vastly appealing that the film could hardly fail to please. Thurber's Mitty personifies all the daydreaming armchair adventurers of the world, and Kaye's portrayal touched numberless people.

207

Virgina Mayo and Danny Kaye.

In the Ken Englund-Everett Freeman screenplay Mitty is a milquetoast who is dominated by his mother (Fay Bainter) and who works as a proof-reader for a pulp-magazine publisher. Whether he is driving his car, sitting at his desk, or being nagged by his mother or his girlfriend (Ann Rutherford), Mitty's mind keeps slipping away into fantasies of heroism. He becomes the captain of a windjammer, guiding his stricken vessel through a ferocious gale, a riverboat gambler of great aplomb and verve, a brilliant surgeon performing an impossible operation, an RAF fighter pilot besting the Luftwaffe, a Western gunfighter of great renown, and the world's leading fashion designer, Anatol of Paris. In many of these flights of fancy the same beautiful blonde (Virginia Mayo) clings to him in devotion.

One day on the train to work he sees exactly such a girl, and she pleads with him for help. She tells him that she is being pursued by villains, and Mitty has only to look over his shoulder to find that she is telling the truth. He becomes involved in antics that end with his bringing to justice a gang of crooks on the trail of buried art treasures. Mitty's success gives him the courage to quiet his mother, free himself from his shrewish girlfriend, and take up with the blonde girl of his dreams.

James Thurber admired the clever dream sequences of the film but denied any responsibility for the rest. However, the movie is a tour de force for Danny Kaye, who fully realized that in playing Walter Mitty he was giving expression to one of the most common of all human tendencies—the drift into fantasy caused by a discontent with reality.

Thurston Hall, Fay Bainter, Danny Kaye and Boris Karloff.

208

Anatole of Paris.

Robert Ryan and Sam Levene.

Crossfire

1947

An RKO-Radio Production; produced by Adrian Scott; directed by Edward Dmytryk; screenplay by John Paxton, based on the novel *The Brick Foxhole,* by Richard Brooks; photographed by J. Roy Hunt; musical score by Roy Webb; running time, 86 minutes.

Cast: Robert Young (*Captain Finlay*), Robert Mitchum (*Sergeant Peter Keeley*), Robert Ryan (*Montgomery*), Gloria Grahame (*Ginny Tremaine*), Paul Kelly (*the Man*), Sam Levene (*Joseph Samuels*), Jacqueline White (*Mary Mitchell*), Steve Brodie (*Floyd Bowers*), George Cooper (*Arthur Mitchell*), Richard Benedict (*Bill Williams*), Richard Powers (*Detective*), William Phipps (*Leroy*), Lex Barker (*Harry*).

The first Hollywood film to tackle anti-Semitism was *Gentleman's Agreement* (1947), but before that expensive Fox property reached completion RKO-Radio made and released *Crossfire*, dealing with the same topic in a tougher and more convincing manner. *Gentleman's Agreement* now seems tame and dated. *Crossfire* doesn't, because apart from its theme it is also a stylishly dark and exciting crime picture.

Richard Brooks wrote his novel *The Brick Foxhole* while serving in the marine corps, and producer Adrian Scott persuaded RKO to buy the book and change its thematic point. Brooks had written about a man who is beaten to death by three soldiers because he is a homosexual, and Scott thought it would be more trenchant and timely if the crime were committed because of anti-Semitism. Brooks agreed to the change, and John Paxton prepared his fine screenplay.

The central figure of *Crossfire* is a sadistic bully of a soldier named Montgomery (Robert Ryan) who quietly seethes with contempt for people of various creeds. In a drunken rage he brutally beats a Jew (Sam Levene) and leaves him to die. Two of his buddies are with Montgomery, but they are too drunk to realize fully what has happened.

The police investigation, led by Captain Finlay (Robert Young), pieces together the facts of the crime from the hazy recollections of one of the men (George Cooper), and when the other man (Steve Brodie) shows signs of cracking under the interrogation Montgomery kills him.

The shrewd killer lies his way out of the investigation, although his army acquaintances are fairly certain of his guilt. One of them, Sergeant Keeley (Robert Mitchum), takes it upon himself to dig up incriminating evidence, and in cooperation with the police he lays a trap that causes Montgomery to reveal himself. In trying to escape Montgomery is shot to death.

Crossfire deservedly won the respect of critics and the public and brought Robert Ryan to justified acclaim. Ryan had met Richard Brooks while serving with the marines, and after reading his book told Brooks that if it were ever filmed he would like to play Montgomery. He played the part so well that he later came to regret it. *Crossfire* gave Ryan an identification with screen villainy that he did not appreciate. Of his own films, Ryan's favorite was *The Set-up* (1949), a tragic story of a boxer past his prime.

210

George Cooper, Robert Mitchum and Robert Young.

Robert Mitchum and Robert Young.

Robert Mitchum, Robert Ryan and Robert Young.

211

Clark Gable, Ava Gardner and Edward Arnold.

The Hucksters

1947

An MGM Production; produced by Arthur Hornblow, Jr.; directed by Jack Conway; screenplay by Luther Davis, based on the novel by Frederic Wakeman, adapted by Edward Chodorov and George Wells; photographed by Harold Rossen; musical score by Lennie Hayton; running time, 115 minutes.

Cast: Clark Gable (*Vic Norman*), Deborah Kerr (*Mrs. Dorrance*), Sydney Greenstreet (*Evans*), Adolphe Menjou (*Mr. Kimberley*), Ava Gardner (*Jean Ogilvie*), Keenan Wynn (*Buddy Hare*), Edward Arnold (*Dave Lash*), Aubrey Mather (*Valet*), Richard Garmes (*Cooke*), Frank Albertson (*Max Herman*), Douglas Fowley (*George Gaver*), Clinton Sundberg (*Michael Michaelson*), Gloria Holden (*Mrs. Kimberley*), Connie Gilchrist (*Betty*).

After the war, Clark Gable was never able to fully recapture the popularity he had enjoyed before. He admitted that after three years as an officer with the Army Air Corps, including a half dozen combat missions as an air gunner, the world of picture making no longer seemed as vital and totally absorbing to him. MGM's first postwar assignment for Gable was *Adventure* (1946), a limp romantic comedy that co-starred him with Greer Garson but pleased neither its actors nor the public.

Gable did better by his next film, *The Hucksters,* a satire on the advertising business. Some of the sting of Frederic Wakeman's novel was missing in the film, and liberties were taken in widening the romantic interests, but enough of the original remained to give viewers an honest, jolting insight into the rough world of promotion-mad American ad men.

212

Clark Gable and Deborah Kerr.

Clark Gable, Ava Gardner, Deborah Kerr, Gloria Holden and Adolphe Menjou.

When Vic Norman (Gable) returns from war service to resume his career in advertising, he takes a job with Kimberley Towers, one of the top agencies. Mr. Kimberley (Adolphe Menjou) is having trouble with his biggest client, Evan Llewellyn Evans (Sydney Greenstreet), the manufacturer of Beautee Soap. Kimberley assigns Vic to the account, and his first job is to persuade Mrs. Dorrence (Deborah Kerr), the beautiful English widow of an American general, to pose for an ad.

In the course of the persuasion he falls in love with her, and her moral standards gradually cause Vic to reassess his own.

His promotions for Evans are successful, and he signs a beautiful singer (Ava Gardner) and a comedian (Keenan Wynn) to do radio shows and recordings for Beautee Soap. But when the pleased Evans offers him a high position with the company, Vic declines. He tells Evans that he wants no part of the "dirty" world of Beautee Soap and that he wants to try a new way of life with his English lady.

Gable's role in *The Hucksters* was perfectly suited to his no-nonsense masculine image, and it probably helped him feel better about his career. Of great aid to the film was Sydney Greenstreet, as the tough and slightly perverse manufacturer.

This was also the picture in which Deborah Kerr made her Hollywood debut. The genteel Briton had already been a movie star for six years, but with an MGM contract and some excellent films, her popularity deservedly increased.

214

Clark Gable and Sydney Greenstreet.

Brian Donlevy, Millard Mitchell, Victor Mature and Karl Malden.

Kiss of Death

1947

A 20th Century-Fox Production; produced by Fred Kohlmar; directed by Henry Hathaway; screenplay by Ben Hecht and Charles Lederer, based on a story by Eleazar Lipsky; photographed by Norbert Brodine; musical score by David Buttolph; running time, 98 minutes.

Cast: Victor Mature (*Nick Bianco*), Brian Donlevy (*D'Angelo*), Coleen Gray (*Nettie*), Richard Widmark (*Tommy Udo*), Taylor Holmes (*Earl Howser*), Howard Smith (*Warden*), Robert Keith (*Judge*), Karl Malden (*Sergeant William Cullen*), Anthony Ross (*Williams*), Mildred Dunnock (*Ma Rizzo*), Millard Mitchell (*Max Schulte*), Temple Texas (*Blondie*), J. Scott Smart (*Skeets*), Jay Jostyn (*District Attorney*).

Victor Mature's performance in *My Darling Clementine* earned him the right to be taken more seri-

ously as an actor—certainly as something more than beefcake. He justified Fox's confidence with a convincing portrait of a reluctant criminal in *Kiss of Death.* Mature was helped by the fine script of Ben Hecht and Charles Lederer and the tough direction of Henry Hathaway.

Two years previously Hathaway had shown Hollywood what could be achieved by working on actual locations, with the semidocumentary spy thriller *The House on 92nd Street,* and when he was assigned *Kiss of Death* he insisted on shooting in New York City. This lent the film a startling aura of authenticity, and thereafter most crime movies with New York settings were photographed in the city.

The central figure in *Kiss of Death* is a smalltime criminal, Nick Bianco (Mature), who would prefer to be legitimate but who feels that fate has conspired to keep him on the wrong side of the law (his father was killed by the police in a holdup

216

Brian Donlevy, Richard Widmark and Victor Mature.

Victor Mature and Coleen Gray.

shooting, and Nick has grown up as a petty thief). He robs a jewelry store on Christmas Eve, claiming it as his only means of providing for his wife and children, but he is caught and jailed.

Nick is sentenced to twenty years, but an assistant district attorney (Brian Donlevy) offers to lessen the term if Nick will inform on his accomplices. He refuses but changes his mind when he learns that his wife has committed suicide and his children have been sent to an orphanage.

One of the thugs on whom Nick is persuaded to inform is a vicious psychopath, Tommy Udo (Richard Widmark), but Udo escapes conviction and thereafter terrorizes Nick and his family in retaliation. In desperation, Nick sets himself as bait in a trap to lure Udo into open action. The ruse works, and Udo is caught, but only after Nick has been severely wounded. He recovers in a hospital and hopes his future will be free of crime.

Kiss of Death is the picture that brought Richard Widmark to the screen. He had spent several years in the New York theaters and made a name for himself in radio drama, but with this arresting debut his future in films was assured. In discussing the film for *Time,* James Agee claimed that much of the fright and suspense was due to Widmark's Tommy Udo. Wrote Agee, "He is a rather frail fellow with maniacal eyes, who uses a sinister kind of falsetto baby talk laced with tittering laughs. It is clear that murder is one of the kindest things he is capable of." Indeed—this was the film in which Widmark pushed a wheelchair-bound old lady headlong down a flight of stairs. A seven-year contract followed.

Richard Conte and James Stewart.

Call Northside 777

1948

A 20th Century-Fox Production; produced by Otto Lang; directed by Henry Hathaway; screenplay by Jerome Cady and Jay Dratler, based on articles by James P. McGuire, adapted by Leonard Hoffman and Quentin Reynolds; photographed by Joe MacDonald; musical score by Alfred Newman; running time, 111 minutes.

Cast: James Stewart (*McNeal*), Richard Conte (*Frank Wiecek*), Lee J. Cobb (*Brian Kelly*), Helen Walker (*Laura McNeal*), Betty Garde (*Wanda Skutnik*), Kasia Orzazewski (*Tillie*), Joanne de Bergh (*Helen Wiecek-Rayska*), Howard Smith (*Palmer*), Moroni Olsen (*Parole Board Chairman*), John McIntire (*Sam Faxon*), Paul Harvey (*Martin Burns*), George Tyne (*Tomek Zaleska*), Richard Bishop (*Warden*), Otto Waldis (*Boris*), Michael Chapin (*Frank, Jr.*), E. G. Marshall (*Rayska*).

James Stewart's luck in postwar Hollywood was greater than that of Clark Gable. Like Gable he had long been an MGM star and had served with distinction in the army air corps, but unlike Gable he was very interested in his career. The astute Stewart declined MGM's offer to return to their fold and decided instead to freelance and pick his own projects.

In his first two films after having been away from Hollywood for five years—*It's a Wonderful Life* (1946) and *Magic Town* (1947)—he resumed the genial, homespun image for which he had formerly been popular, but with *Call Northside 777* Stewart became tougher and more tenacious. This was also the next film in line for director Henry Hathaway after *Kiss of Death,* and again Hathaway insisted on genuine locations and a gritty kind of reality—this time in Chicago.

Call Northside 777, based on a true story, is the

James Stewart, E. G. Marshall, Michael Chapin and Joanne de Bergh.

account of a newspaperman's dogged attempts to clear a falsely convicted man. McNeal (Stewart) is asked by his editor (Lee J. Cobb) to follow up a small ad that has appeared in the paper. The ad offers a reward for any information concerning a murder case of a dozen years before.

McNeal finds that the ad was placed by an impoverished scrubwoman, the mother of the convicted man. He is touched by her sincerity and goes to see her son, Frank Wiecek (Richard Conte), who seems intent on serving his sentence and asks McNeal not to pursue the matter. McNeal feels he should comply, but both the editor and McNeal's wife (Helen Walker) believe that he should continue.

The more he digs into the matter the more he becomes convinced of Wiecek's innocence. Finally he discovers discrepancies in the evidence of a female witness and inaccuracies in police records concerning the time of arrest and indictment. With this information McNeal is able to free Wiecek.

Once again Hathaway's use of actual locations proved powerfully effective. *Call Northside 777* involved the Polish community of Chicago and employed many local citizens, but James Stewart's performance provides the backbone of the film. His acting skill had increased with his determination to find good properties, and it would continue to increase with a string of entertaining movies all through the fifties—a period in which many other stars floundered and drifted.

James Stewart and Helen Walker.

John McIntire to the left of James Stewart and Paul Harvey to the right.

221

Ronald Colman and Signe Hasso.

A Double Life

1947

A Universal-International Production; produced by Michael Kanin; directed by George Cukor; screenplay by Ruth Gordon and Garson Kanin; photographed by Milton Krasner; musical score by Miklos Rozsa; running time, 104 minutes.

Cast: Ronald Colman (*Anthony John*), Signe Hasso (*Brita*), Edmond O'Brien (*Bill Friend*), Shelley Winters (*Pat Kroll*), Ray Collins (*Victor Donjan*), Philip Loeb (*Max Lasker*), Millard Mitchell (*Al Cooley*), Joe Sawyer (*Ray Bonner*), Charles La Torre (*Stellini*), Whit Bissell (*Doctor Stauffer*), John Drew Colt (*Stage Manager*), Peter Thompson (*Assistant*), Elizabeth Dunne (*Gladys*), Alan Edmiston (*Rex*).

Ronald Colman won a richly deserved Oscar for his performance in *A Double Life*. It came near the end of his distinguished career (he died in 1958), and it was an appropriate token of recognition for all that he had been to Hollywood. In this picture he played a distinguished actor—but an actor far removed from his own experience. The actor in *A Double Life* hid depression and despair beneath his smooth exterior. Colman himself had nothing to hide. He was a thoroughly sane and civilized gentleman, but he was well aware that his profession had destroyed the souls of some of its followers.

In writing a story about the theater and its people, Garson Kanin and Ruth Gordon were also acutely aware of their subject, as was George Cukor in directing it. Because of all this, *A Double Life* has an air of absolute authority and conviction. Even for those with little interest in the theater, it is an arresting and disturbing story.

Anthony John (Colman) is one of Broadway's top attractions, a handsome gentleman-actor along the lines of John Barrymore and a veteran of his craft. His forte is classical drama, and he has an affinity for *Othello*. Seemingly affable and pleasantly cooperative with his fellow workers, John is actually lonely and frequently withdrawn. His ex-wife, Brita (Signe Hasso), still loves and understands him, even though she has been subjected to his cruelties, and they still act together.

Signe Hasso and Ronald Colman.

Ronald Colman and Shelley Winters.

In his loneliness John indulges in a relationship with a waitress (Shelley Winters), a commonly attractive but not very bright girl. She is fascinated by the actor and later afraid of him—with good reason, for Anthony John is bordering on dementia and increasingly unable to differentiate between his own psyche and the those of the characters he plays.

Othello becomes his downfall. In a performance of the play, with Brita as Desdemona, John's mind tricks him. He suddenly believes that he really is the Moor, and when Brita cries Desdemona's plea for mercy, "Banish me Lord, but kill me not," she knows she is speaking the line in earnestness. He does indeed kill her.

A Double Life was a tour de force for Ronald Colman and the high point in his career. Two years later he made a feeble comedy, *Champagne for Caesar,* and he had cameo roles in *The Story of Mankind* and *Around the World in Eighty Days* (1956), as well as a television series, "The Halls of Ivy." But this was all rather the work of a man amusing himself in retirement. Perhaps it is best to regard *A Double Life* as the true climax in the career of Ronald Colman.

224

Irene Dunne, Rudy Vallee and Oscar Homolka.

I Remember Mama

1948

An RKO-Radio Production; produced and directed by George Stevens; screenplay by DeWitt Bodeen, based on the play by John Van Druten, from the novel by Kathryn Forbes; photographed by Robert Swink; musical score by Roy Webb; running time, 134 minutes.

Cast: Irene Dunne (*Mama*), Barbara Bel Geddes (*Katrin*), Oscar Homolka (*Uncle Chris*), Philip Dorn (*Papa*), Sir Cedric Hardwicke (*Mr. Hyde*), Edgar Bergen (*Mr. Thorkelson*), Rudy Vallee (*Doctor Johnson*), Barbara O'Neil (*Jessie Brown*), Florence Bates (*Florence Dana Moorhead*), Peggy McIntyre (*Christine*), June Hedin (*Dagmar*), Steve Brown (*Nels*), Ellen Corby (*Aunt Trina*), Hope Landin (*Aunt Jenny*), Edith Evanson (*Aunt Sigrid*), Tommy Ivo (*Cousin Arne*).

Kathryn Forbes's pleasant novel of reminiscences of her childhood and her family in San Francisco was adroitly adapted by John Van Druten into a stage play and then transferred into a screenplay by DeWitt Bodeen. Nothing was lost in any of the transitions, and in the hands of producer-director George Stevens, the most painstaking of all Hollywood filmmakers, the movie version is a delight. Most delightful of all is Irene Dunne as Mama. Her portrayal is an idealization of motherhood but a thoroughly believable one and a tribute to the skill of an actress who had the rare ability to combine beauty with warm humor.

The characters in *I Remember Mama* are working-class Norwegian Americans, and they are a genial lot. Mama and Papa (Philip Dorn) have three daughters and a son, and the eldest daughter, Katrin (Barbara Bel Geddes), is the narrator. She keeps a diary and records the ups and downs, the comings and goings, of her relatives, and these recollections are voiced from the present, with the incidents illustrated in the form of flashbacks.

The family lives in a large old house on Larkin Street and cheerily struggles to make ends meet. One of the main members is Uncle Chris (Oscar Homolka), blustering and demanding but a pillar of wisdom in times of stress, which seem to be fre-

quent. Their boarder is Mr. Hyde (Sir Cedric Hardwicke), an old English gentleman who reads to the family in the evenings. Among the regular visitors are three formidable aunts, Mr. Thorkelson (Edgar Bergen), a neighbor who runs a funeral parlor, and Doctor Johnson (Rudy Vallee), who ministers to Uncle Chris as the old man dies and to impish little Christine (Peggy McIntyre) when she suffers from a mastoid condition.

Much of the story takes place within the house, a little world unto itself, and whenever the members of the family are seen on the street they appear eager to get home—which is understandable in view of its security-blanket atmosphere.

The role of Mama is not a greatly difficult one for a competent actress, but when played by an exceptional talent, it glows. Such was the case with Irene Dunne. With braided blonde hair and just the right amount of Norwegian accent, she appeared as a good-natured woman communicating both strength and gentleness in her concern for her family. Everyone should have such a mother.

Philip Dorn and Irene Dunne.

Irene Dunne, Steve Brown, Philip Dorn and Ellen Corby.

Steve Brown, Irene Dunne and Peggy McIntire.

Butch Jenkins, Selena Royle, Mickey Rooney, Walter Huston, Agnes Moorehead, Frank Morgan and Shirley Johns.

Summer Holiday

1948

An MGM Production; produced by Arthur Freed; directed by Rouben Mamoulian; screenplay by Frances Goodrich and Albert Hackett, based on the play *Ah, Wilderness!* by Eugene O'Neill; photographed in Technicolor by Charles Schoenbaum; songs by Harry Warren and Ralph Blane; musical direction by Lennie Hayton; running time, 92 minutes.

Cast: Mickey Rooney (*Richard Miller*), Gloria De Haven (*Muriel McComber*), Walter Huston (*Nat Miller*), Frank Morgan (*Uncle Sid*), Butch Jenkins (*Tommy*), Marilyn Maxwell (*Belle*), Agnes Moorehead (*Cousin Lily*), Selena Royle (*Mrs. Miller*), Michael Kirby (*Arthur Miller*), Shirley Johns (*Mildred*), Hal Hackett (*Wint*), Ann Francis (*Elsie Rand*), John Alexander (*Mr. McComber*), Virginia Brissac (*Miss Hawley*), Howard Freeman (*Mr. Peabody*), Alice MacKenzie (*Mrs. McComber*), Ruth Brady (*Christal*).

Summer Holiday is an exceptional musical, full of charm and humor and gaiety, and yet it was not greatly successful. This musicalization of Eugene O'Neill's *Ah, Wilderness!* employs subtlety and genuine artistry in re-creating the life-style in a small Connecticut town around the turn of the century. The movements in the film are fluid, the sets and costumes are exact, and the use of color is as skillful as it is pleasing.

The credit for all this belongs to the estimable Rouben Mamoulian, whose Hollywood career was not nearly so fulfilling as it should have been, mostly because he demanded to do things his way at a time when directors were required to follow the instructions of the studios. Mamoulian's last film before this was *Rings on Her Fingers* (1942), and it would be 1957 before he returned to Hollywood, to make *Silk Stockings*.

Between 1943 and 1947 Mamoulian won great approval with his staging of such Broadway musi-

cals as *St. Louis Woman, Oklahoma!* and *Carousel.*
That same kind of high stylishness is apparent in
Summer Holiday.

O'Neill claimed that the quality of *Ah, Wilderness!* depended on atmosphere, sentiment, and "an
exact mood of a dead past." Ralph Blane's lyrics
and Harry Warren's music help the film achieve
precisely this. The opening song, "It's Our Home
Town," sets the feeling of pride as newspaper editor
Nat Miller (Walter Huston) sings happily about
his town, and as the scene switches to his home his
son Richard (Mickey Rooney) continues the lyric
to state his case.

Richard wins over his hesitant girlfriend, Muriel
(Gloria De Haven), by singing "Afraid to Fall in
Love" and then whisks her on a jaunty dance
through the park.

On an automobile outing the family sings about
its "Stanley Steamer," and on "Independence Day"
there is no doubt about patriotism. The cocky
young Richard gets cut to size when he tries to flirt
with dance-hall Belle (Marilyn Maxwell), and she
tells him, "I Think You're the Sweetest Kid I've
Ever Known" and scares the life out of him.
Richard eagerly retreats to Muriel and decides to
marry her and become a part of the solid, respectable set of Danville, Connecticut.

In its style and setting *Summer Holiday* can be
compared with Minnelli's *Meet Me in St. Louis.*
Although lacking the total impact of the earlier
musical, the Mamoulian picture is a thorough
delight. Appreciation for its quality continues to
grow with time.

Mickey Rooney and Gloria De Haven.

Mickey Rooney and Marilyn Maxwell.

Gloria De Haven, Mickey Rooney and Agnes Moorehead.

Frances Dee and Joel McCrea.

Four Faces West

Joseph Calleia, Frances Dee and Joel McCrea.

1948

An Enterprise Production, released by United Artists; produced by Harry Sherman; directed by Alfred E. Green; screenplay by Graham Baker and Teddi Sherman, adapted by William and Milarde Brent from the novel *Paso por Aqui,* by Eugene Manlove Rhodes; photographed by Russell Harlan; musical score by Paul Sawtell; running time, 90 minutes.

Cast: Joel McCrea (*Ross McEwen*), Frances Dee (*Fay Hollister*), Charles Bickford (*Pat Garrett*), Joseph Calleia (*Monte Marquez*), William Conrad (*Sheriff Egan*), William Garralaga (*Florencia*), Raymond Largey (*Doctor Elridge*), John Parrish (*Prenger*), Dan White (*Clint Waters*), Davison Clark (*Burnett*), Eva Novak (*Mrs. Winston*), George McDonald (*Winston Boy*), Housely Stevenson (*Anderson*), Sam Flint (*Storekeeper*), Forrest Taylor (*Conductor*).

In the second half of his screen career Joel McCrea devoted himself to Westerns. All through the thirties and the early forties he had been a leading man in sundry dramas and light comedies but after making *The Virginian* in 1946, he appeared in only one non-Western. This was a murder mystery made in England called *Rough Shoot* (1952), and from its title anyone not having seen it could well assume it to be a Western.

McCrea retired in 1962 after making the excellent *Ride the High Country* and ignored all further offers of film work. He could afford to—aside from his screen career, McCrea had long been a cattle rancher. The proceeds from his vast acreage around Camarillo, California, made him a millionaire.

Among his best Westerns is a small gem called *Four Faces West,* which enjoys the distinction of being the only Western ever made without a shot fired.

What *Four Faces West* lacks in gunpowder it makes up for in its respect for Western ways and its credibility. The original story stems from Eugene Manlove Rhodes, a cowboy who turned novelist and based his yarns on incidents in his own life or those about which he had learned. This one is about Ross McEwen (McCrea), who robs a bank because he needs money to save the family ranch and then leaves the banker with an I.O.U.

He is pursued by Sheriff Pat Garrett (Charles Bickford), and in taking a ride on a train he meets an Eastern nurse, Fay Hollister (Frances Dee), who has accepted a position in a small New Mexico hospital. The two begin to fall in love, but McEwen has no choice but to leave her and continue his escape. He is befriended by a compassionate saloon owner, Monte Marquez (Joseph Calleia), who realizes that McEwen is no bandit at heart.

McEwen makes his way across the desert, but in stopping for water at a small ranch he discovers a Mexican family stricken by diphtheria. The father pleads for help to save the lives of his children, and in answering the plea McEwen exhausts himself.

It is here that Garrett finds him and arrests him, but Garrett feels certain that McEwen's fate in the hands of the law will be lenient. Garrett lets him say goodbye to Fay and Monte, and Monte assures her that McEwen is a gentleman and that there is no doubt of his return.

Joel McCrea, no doubt because of his secondary career as a rancher, was a splendid horseman, and in his quiet, dignified, masculine manner he was an ideal movie Westerner.

Four Faces West shows him to great advantage, as it does his wife, the graceful Frances Dee.

Joseph Calleia, Charles Bickford, Dan White and Joel McCrea.

Marlene Dietrich and Jean Arthur.

A Foreign Affair

1948

A Paramount Production; produced by Charles Brackett; directed by Billy Wilder; screenplay by Charles Brackett, Billy Wilder, and Richard L. Breen, based on a story by David Shaw; photographed by Charles B. Lang, Jr.; musical score and songs by Frederick Hollander; running time, 116 minutes.

Cast: Jean Arthur (*Phoebe Frost*), Marlene Dietrich (*Erika von Schluetow*), John Lund (*Captain John Pringle*), Millard Mitchell (*Colonel Rufus J. Plummer*), Bill Murphy (*Joe*), Stanley Prager (*Mike*), Peter von Zerneck (*Hans Otto Birgel*), Raymond Bond (*Pennecott*), Boyd Davis (*Griffin*), Robert Malcolm (*Kraus*), Charles Meredith (*Yandell*), Michael Raffeto (*Salvatore*), James Larmore (*Lieutenant Hornby*), Damian O'Flynn (*Lieutenant Colonel*), Frank Fenton (*Major*), William Neff (*Lieutenant Lee Thompson*), Harland Tucker (*General McAndrew*), George Carleton (*General Finney*), Gordon Jones, Freddie Steele (*Military Policemen*).

Billy Wilder's films are etched by his mordant sense of humor and his uncompromising desire to tell the truth as he sees it. Consequently, some parties take offense at them. Insurance companies didn't care much for *Double Indemnity,* liquor manufacturers objected to *The Lost Weekend,* and in 1951 Wilder so offended the newspaper industry with *Ace in the Hole* that the film's publicity campaign was severely curtailed.

With *A Foreign Affair* Wilder incurred the disapproval of the U.S. Government, particularly the Defense Department, because he acutely satirized their occupation administration in postwar Berlin. Many of the exteriors were shot in Berlin in the winter of 1947–48, and since Wilder was a product of that city his views of Germans and Americans can be taken as fairly accurate. However, his main point, that "people are people," seemed to strike some 1948 moviegoers as rather radical.

The story revolves around a congresswoman, Phoebe Frost (Jean Arthur); a German aristocrat turned entertainer, Erika Von Schluetow (Marlene

Jean Arthur.

Dietrich); and an army captain, John Pringle (John Lund). Miss Frost heads a delegation to investigate stories of moral malaise and fraternization with the Germans among the thousands of American soldiers in Berlin. She seeks out Captain Pringle, to give him a birthday cake from a girl-friend. He takes it to the nearest black market to trade it for a mattress, which he gives to his current lady love, Erika.

Erika's background is Nazi tainted, but Pringle has doctored her papers so she can remain in the city and earn a living singing in a nightclub.

Phoebe Frost creates tremors with her probing and homes in on Erika—but the army prefers Pringle to keep up his affair with her because one of her ex-lovers is a Nazi at large.

The Nazi turns up at the nightclub and is shot, and Erika is hauled away by the army, doubtless to survive. After various enlightening experiences, Phoebe has her mind broadened and her heart opened by Pringle.

A Foreign Affair is a searing look at the human comedy and vastly amusing. In Jean Arthur and Marlene Dietrich, Wilder had the services of two exceptionally adroit performers, and for Dietrich, sardonically chanting songs like "Black Market" and "Illusions" in a cellar nightclub, it must have seemed a little like *The Blue Angel* revisited.

John Lund, Jean Arthur and Millard Mitchell.

Walter Brennan, John Wayne and Mickey Kuhn.

Red River

John Wayne and Montgomery Clift.

1948

A Monterey-United Artists Production; produced and directed by Howard Hawks; screenplay by Borden Chase and Charles Schnee, based on a story by Chase; photographed by Russell Harlan; musical score by Dimitri Tiomkin; running time, 125 minutes.

Cast: John Wayne (*Tom Dunson*), Montgomery Clift (*Matthew Garth*), Joanne Dru (*Tess Millay*), Walter Brennan (*Groot Nadine*), Coleen Gray (*Fen*), John Ireland (*Cherry Valance*), Noah Beery, Jr. (*Buster McGee*), Harry Carey, Sr. (*Mr. Millville*), Harry Carey, Jr. (*Dan Latimer*), Paul Fix (*Teeler Yacy*), Mickey Kuhn (*Matt as a boy*), Chief Yowlachie (*Quo*), Ivan Parry (*Bunk Kenneally*), Ray Hyke (*Walt Jergens*), Hank Worden (*Simms*), Dan White (*Laredo*), Paul Fiero (*Fernandez*), William Self (*Wounded Wrangler*), Hal Taliaferro (*Old Leather*), Tom Tyler (*a Quitter*), Lane Chandler (*Colonel*), Glenn Strange (*Naylor*), Shelley Winters (*Dance-hall Girl*).

John Wayne's identification with Westerns dates from *The Big Trail* in 1930, and although he has appeared in other kinds of pictures, his image is now as much a part of the American West as Monument Valley. Most of Wayne's Westerns for John Ford are classics, but in 1948 he made one for Howard Hawks that is almost in a class of its own. *Red River* is a hard, crusty Western, lacking Ford's sentimental touches and depicting the life of cattle-driving cowboys as the bleak, severe experience it must truly have been. The very masculine quality of Hawks's work is well suited to making Westerns, and in writer Bordon Chase he had an authority on the West. In this film Hawks also benefited from Russell Harlan's photography and from one of Dimitri Tiomkin's best Western scores.

It can be said that *Red River* has nothing new to say about the old West, but in the hands of Hawks and his company it tells its tale with force and style.

Thomas Dunson (Wayne) is a Texas rancher who carves a small empire after the Civil War. He is a tough, single-minded, uncompromising kind of man and somewhat at odds with his gentler, intelligent foster son, Matthew (Montgomery Clift).

With the market for beef in the South depressed, Dunson decides to take his cattle north to Kansas and the railhead that serves the North and the East. In this Dunson is a pioneer, the first rancher to use what will become known as the Chisholm Trail.

The massive cattle drive is long, laborious, and dangerous. Dunson drives his men almost as hard as the cattle, and several of them desert. He goes after them, brings them back, and tells them they are to die. Garth now openly defies him, and the two are driven apart by their opposing views.

Later, after the drive has been completed, the two face each other. Dunson slaps Matthew, but the son refuses to fight. Dunson keep slapping him until Matthew's temper breaks and he finally hits back. The savage brawl clears the anger out of both of them and signals a new relationship, with Dunson making Matthew a full partner in his business.

Wayne is perfect as the flinty, self-made Dunson, and in his second film appearance Montgomery Clift made a strong impression with his contrastingly quiet, subjective performance. Red River is the cattle-drive picture *par excellence*.

Hal Taliaferro, John Ireland, John Wayne, Hank Worden, Montgomery Clift, Walter Brennan, Chief Yowlachie and Ivan Parry (kneeling).

Joanne Dru and John Wayne.

Montgomery Clift and John Wayne.

Sorry Wrong Number

1948

A Paramount Production; produced by Anatole Litvak and Hal Wallis; directed by Anatole Litvak; screenplay by Lucille Fletcher, based on her radio drama; photographed by Sol Polito; musical score by Franz Waxman; running time, 89 minutes.

Cast: Barbara Stanwyck (*Leona Stevenson*), Burt Lancaster (*Henry Stevenson*), Ann Richards (*Sally Lord*), Wendell Corey (*Doctor Alexander*), Harold Vermilyea (*Waldo Evans*), Ed Begley (*James Cotterill*), Leif Erickson (*Fred Lord*), William Conrad (*Morano*), Jimmy Hunt (*Peter Lord*), Dorothy Nuemann (*Miss Jenkins*).

Burt Lancaster and Barbara Stanwyck.

Lucille Fletcher's half-hour radio play "Sorry Wrong Number" had served as a one-woman tour de force for Agnes Moorehead in its several broadcasts, but by the Hollywood yardsticks of 1948 Moorehead was not considered a sufficiently potent name to carry a major film.

The plum went to the highly capable Barbara Stanwyck, who had starred in at least two films a year throughout the forties but who felt that she needed a particularly good vehicle to arrest the decline of her popularity. Her performance brought her an Academy Award nomination, her fourth, but the film failed to make a great impression because it clearly showed Miss Fletcher's difficulty in developing a short story into a long one. As in the radio play, the finest moments of the film come in its last ten minutes, as a woman hopelessly caught in a trap awaits her inevitable death.

Leona Stevenson (Stanwyck) is a spoiled society woman given to hypochondria and other neuroses. A series of flashbacks establishes that her relationship with her hard-driving businessman father (Ed Begley) is a basic cause of her malcontented nature and that it is mostly because of her wealth that she has landed a young and virile husband, Henry (Burt Lancaster).

Henry is shady in his business dealings and gets himself involved with crooks. His luck turns bad, and he finds himself desperately in need of money to save his life. The only money he can possibly get is the insurance on his wife's life, and he arranges for her murder.

Leona has become a self-induced invalid and spends most of her time in bed, talking at length on the telephone to whoever she can call. The switchboard girls of the telephone company have come to know her as an ungracious pest.

One evening Leona finds herself plugged into a wrong line, and she listens in horror as two men discuss plans to kill a woman. It gradually dawns upon her that she is the woman and that the killing is only minutes away. Her frantic calls to the operator to reach the police result in confusion—she has cried wolf too often—and her husband, whom she tries to reach by phone, has no intention of being reached or coming to her aid.

The direction of the polished Anatole Litvak creates the necessary mood of mounting tension, assisted by Franz Waxman's music and the photography of the masterly Sol Polito. But most of all, Barbara Stanwyck's acting, in a not very sympathetic part, makes this film memorable.

Barbara Stanwyck and Burt Lancaster.

Jane Wyman and Charles Bickford.

Jane Wyman and Lew Ayres.

Johnny Belinda

1948

A Warner Bros. Production; produced by Jerry Wald; directed by Jean Negulesco; screenplay by Irmgard Von Cube and Allen Vincent, based on the play by Elmer Harris; photographed by Ted McCord; musical score by Max Steiner; running time, 102 minutes.

Cast: Jane Wyman (*Belinda McDonald*), Lew Ayres (*Doctor Robert Richardson*), Charles Bickford (*Black McDonald*), Agnes Moorehead (*Aggie McDonald*), Stephan McNally (*Locky McCormick*), Jan Sterling (*Stella McGuire*), Rosalind Ivan (*Mrs. Poggety*), Dan Seymour (*Pacquet*), Mabel Paige (*Mrs. Lutz*), Ida Moore (*Mrs. McKee*), Alan Napier (*Defense Attorney*), Monte Blue (*Ben*), Douglas Kennedy (*Mountie*), James Craven (*Interpreter*).

Jane Wyman began her Hollywood career in the mid-thirties as a song-and-dance girl and labored in many Warners movies over a ten-year period as a light-comedic actress. She eventually found this image tiresome and left Warners to find better and more serious roles at other studios. After her appearances in *The Lost Weekend, The Yearling* (1946), and *Magic Town* (1957), Warners was prepared to take her more seriously and offered her the lead in *Johnny Belinda*.

This was very much a departure from anything the actress had ever tackled, requiring her to portray a simple, repressed deaf-mute. The Oscar Miss Wyman won for this performance indicated the esteem of the film industry, and as time passes it becomes even more obvious that this is the highlight of her career and one of the most touching portrayals ever achieved on the American screen.

The play by Elmer Harris was staged on Broadway in 1940 and met with only moderate success. Plays do not always translate well to film, but in this instance it was possible to improve on the original material. The film medium could place the story in the kind of rugged country settings it called for and fully develop the girl's character and her plight.

244

Belinda is the only child of a rough-natured farmer (Charles Bickford), who has never forgiven her because his wife died giving birth to the child. A young doctor (Lew Ayres) takes up practice in the nearby town and educates Belinda in sign language. He also persuades her family to appreciate her intelligence and her sweet nature.

One evening a local swaggerer, Locky McCormick (Stephen McNally), visits Belinda while drunk and rapes her. When the product of this rape is born, the community assumes that the doctor is the father, and he is forced to leave. Belinda's father finally realizes who the culprit is. When he faces McCormick, McCormick kills him and throws the body over a cliff, and the death is assumed to be an accident.

McCormick decides that he wants his child for himself but so terrifies Belinda with his demands that she imagines he wants to harm the child. She shoots and kills McCormick and is put on trial for murder.

Jane Wyman and Stephen McNally.

Charles Bickford, Jane Wyman and Lew Ayres.

The case against her seems complete, but McCormick's wife (Jan Sterling) rises to her defense and admits that her husband was the father of Belinda's child. The court hands down a verdict of self-defense, the townspeople take her into their hearts, and the waiting doctor takes her into his arms.

The locale of the story is the fishing and farming district of Cape Breton Island, Nova Scotia. Since the weather of the distant setting is often severe and usually unpredictable, Warners chose a location in California, the jagged, spectacular coastal area around Fort Bragg and Mendocino, two hundred miles north of San Francisco. Like Cape Breton, this district is subject to fog, winds, and rain, and since the story called for these elements, photographer Ted McCord was able to incorporate them in his remarkable photography. The gentler elements of the story were highlighted by Max Steiner's memorable score. For all that, the crowning achievement of this splendid picture is Jane Wyman's acting.

Errol Flynn, Robert Douglas, Romney Brent and Viveca Lindfors.

Adventures of Don Juan

1949

A Warner Bros. Production; produced by Jerry Wald; directed by Vincent Sherman; screenplay by George Oppenheimer and Harry Kurnitz, based on a story by Herbert Dalmas; photographed in Technicolor by Elwood Bredell; musical score by Max Steiner; running time, 110 minutes.

Cast: Errol Flynn (*Don Juan de Marana*), Viveca Lindfors (*Queen Margaret*), Robert Douglas (*Duke de Lorca*), Alan Hale (*Leporello*), Romney Brent (*King Philip III*), Ann Rutherford (*Doña Elena*), Robert Warwick (*Count de Polan*), Jerry Austin (*Don Sebastian*), Douglas Kennedy (*Don Rodrigo*), Jeanne Shepherd (*Doña Carolotta*), Mary Stuart (*Catherine*), Helen Westcott (*Lady Diana*), Fortunio Bonanova (*Don Serafino*), Aubrey Mather (*Lord Chalmers*), Una O'Connor (*Dueña*), Raymond Burr (*Captain Alvarez*), G. P. Huntley, Jr. (*Catherine's Husband*), David Leonard (*Innkeeper*), Leon Belasco (*Don de Cordoba*), Pedro de Cordoba (*Pachecho*), David Bruce (*Count D'Orsini*), Monte Blue (*Turnkey*), Barbara Bates (*Innkeeper's Daughter*), Harry Lewis (*Innkeeper's Son*).

It was almost inevitable that Warners would eventually star Errol Flynn as Don Juan. Flynn had acquired a decidely phallic reputation, and despite his efforts to establish himself as an actor capable of comedy and drama, the public seemed interested in him only as a dashing, costumed adventurer. He was also a worshiper of John Barrymore, and one of the first great Warners pictures had been Barrymore's *Don Juan* in 1926.

The Flynn version was scheduled to begin shooting in the spring of 1945, but it was immediately beset by union problems. Each attempt to get the project going met with problems, and it was constantly postponed.

Filming actually began late in 1947, but by this time the biggest problem was Flynn. He had worked up a dislike for his employers, and in hedonistically setting out to enjoy life to the hilt, he had severely undermined his health. The wonder is that *Adventures of Don Juan* is as good as it is. Flynn's capers and delays added half a million dollars to the budget.

The film loses no time in making its point—it begins with Don Juan in England, climbing a trellis

to the balcony of a beautiful young woman. Her nobleman husband happens to return prematurely, and the incident results in Don Juan's being sent home in disgrace by the Spanish ambassador.

In Madrid he finds King Philip (Romney Brent) and Queen Margaret (Viveca Lindfors) under the thumb of the Duke de Lorca (Robert Douglas), a prime minister intent on taking over the country. Don Juan offers his services to the crown and is put in charge of the royal fencing academy. He becomes involved in the intrigues of the court, quickly senses the danger to the throne, and finally brings about the fall of de Lorca, killing him in a duel.

The queen, who has been holding back on her feelings for him, asks Don Juan to take her with him as he prepares to leave Madrid. He wisely persuades her that her duty lies with her people, and in company with the faithful Leporello (Alan Hale), he departs to seek adventures elsewhere.

Adventures of Don Juan is Errol Flynn's high-water mark as a swashbuckler. He would make a few more costume pictures, but his failing health and spirit would rob them of vitality. Even here, at thirty-nine, he was tiring, and yet his very air of mocking *Weltschmerz* made his Don Juan amusing and acceptable.

Viveca Lindfors and Errol Flynn.

247

Viveca Lindfors, Romney Brent, Jerry Austen, Robert Douglas and Errol Flynn.

Linda Darnell, Ann Sothern, Jeanne Crain and an unidentified mailman.

A Letter to Three Wives

1949

A 20th Century-Fox Production; produced by Sol C. Siegel; directed and written by Joseph L. Mankiewicz, adapted by Vera Caspary from the novel by John Klempner; photographed by Arthur Miller; musical score by Alfred Newman; running time, 103 minutes.

Cast: Jeanne Crain (*Deborah Bishop*), Linda Darnell (*Lora May Hollingsway*), Ann Sothern (*Rita Phipps*), Kirk Douglas (*George Phipps*), Paul Douglas (*Porter Hollingsway*), Barbara Lawrence (*Babe*), Jeffrey Lynn (*Brad Bishop*), Connie Gilchrist (*Mrs. Finney*), Florence Bates (*Mrs. Manleigh*), Hobart Cavanaugh (*Mr. Manleigh*), Patti Brady (*Kathleen*), Ruth Vivian (*Miss Hawkins*), Thelma Ritter (*Sadie*).

Jeffrey Lynn and Jeanne Crain.

Although marriage has always been material for authors and scenarists, it has usually been depicted as either heaven or hell. In most comedies about marriage the husband is the butt of the jokes. *A Letter to Three Wives* is, thanks to the taste and talent of Joseph L. Mankiewicz, perhaps the wittiest film ever made about marriage, and it focuses most of its attention and critical comment on wives. It does not lacerate these ladies—it gently takes them to task.

The catalyst of the story is a lady named Addie Ross, apparently a close friend of each of the three husbands. She is never seen, but her voice (that of Celeste Holm) gives sufficient narration to set up the characters and situations of the wives.

As the wives are about to set off on a boating trip on the Hudson River as guides to a party of youngsters, a postman delivers a letter to each of them. The letters are from Addie, and the messages have a common theme—by the end of the day Addie will leave the town with the husband of one of the women, but she does not say which. This causes each wife to reflect on her marriage and why she could be losing her husband.

Their recollections are the substance of the film. Deborah Bishop (Jeanne Crain) is overpossessive about her Brad (Jeffrey Lynn) because she came from a lower level of society and has never felt quite secure. Has she clung too tightly? Lora May Hollingsway (Linda Darnell) landed her wealthy

Thelma Ritter, Paul Douglas, Linda Darnell and Connie Gilchrist.

businessman, Porter (Paul Douglas), by taunting him into marriage. Is he now tired of her? Rita Philips (Ann Sothern) has become successful as a writer of radio soap operas while her literate schoolteacher husband, George (Kirk Douglas), insists on following his honest but unremunerative profession. Is he disgusted with her work?

None of the wives turns out to be a loser. The man Addie had chosen to steal was Porter Hollingsway, but he changes his mind because he loves his wife in spite of her exasperating ways. The trauma of the day causes each of the wives to take stock of marriage and change her ways for the better. The acting of the six principals is superb, especially that of Paul Douglas and Kirk Douglas, and Mankiewicz won two Oscars, one for his script and one for his direction. Few other filmmakers have matched his ability to write pungent and intelligent dialogue.

Kirk Douglas and Ann Sothern.

Jennifer Jones and Joseph Cotten.

Portrait of Jennie

1949

A Selznick Production; produced by David O. Selznick; directed by William Dieterle; screenplay by Paul Osborn and Peter Berneis, based on the novel by Robert Nathan; photographed by Joseph August; musical score by Dimitri Tiomkin; running time, 86 minutes.

Cast: Jennifer Jones (*Jennie Appleton*), Joseph Cotten (*Eben Adams*), Ethel Barrymore (*Miss Spinney*), Cecil Kellaway (*Mr. Matthews*), David Wayne (*Gus O'Toole*), Albert Sharpe (*Mr. Moore*), Florence Bates (*Mrs. Jekes*), Lillian Gish (*Mother Mary of Mercy*), Henry Hull (*Eke*), Esther Somers (*Mrs. Bunce*), Maude Simmons (*Clara Morgan*), Felix Bressart (*Doorman*), John Farrell (*Policeman*), Clem Bevans (*Captain Caleb Cobb*), Robert Dudley (*Old Mariner*).

David O. Selznick was much disappointed with his *Portrait of Jennie*, feeling that the enormous amount of money he had spent making it was not apparent on the screen and that as an exercise in romantic fantasy it was less than it should have been. Many critics readily agreed. The public was somewhat kinder, and anyone interested in the art of making movies can look at this one with considerable interest. It suffers, as do other Selznick productions, from being pretentious, especially in a lofty foreword by Ben Hecht, which speaks of the mysteries of infinity, time, and life and death and ends with, "Out of the shadows of knowledge, and out of a painting that hung on a museum wall, comes our story, the truth of which lies not on our screen but in your heart."

Had the film promised less it would have been more enjoyable. It's really a slight story, and Selznick spoiled it by trying to pump it up to epic proportions.

The story concerns a painter, Eben Adams (Joseph Cotten), who meets a young girl in New York's Central Park in the wintertime. Jennie Appleton (Jennifer Jones) is a radiant and rather ethereal youngster, and Adams is greatly affected by her. She sings him a little song, the main lyric of which is, "Where I come from nobody knows—and

where I'm going everything goes. The wind blows, the sea flows—and nobody knows." She leaves after telling him about her parents, who she claims are trapeze artists at Hammerstein's Opera House. Adams later realizes that the Opera House was pulled down long ago.

The two meet several times during the following months, and each time, Jennie seems some years older. Adam's friends watch with curiosity as he paints her portrait and gently scoff at his stories about her.

He discovers that Jennie was once in a convent, and his curiosity leads him to ask the mother superior (Lillian Gish) about Jennie. He learns that Jennie died some years ago in a storm off the coast of Cape Cod. There, on the anniversary of the storm, he sees Jennie for the last time, as she comes to him during a furious gale. They have a few moments together; then she is swept away to her death in the sea.

Jennifer Jones, who by this time was Mrs. Selznick, appears to advantage in *Portrait of Jennie*. She conveys the strange quality of the beautiful, mysterious girl who drifts in and out of the painter's life. Joseph August's photography is especially effective, as is Dimitri Tiomkin's Debussy-based musical score. *Portrait of Jennie* is a flawed canvas but a haunting one.

254

The Great Gatsby

1949

A Paramount Production; produced by Richard Maibaum; directed by Elliott Nugent; screenplay by Cyril Hume and Richard Maibaum, based on the novel by F. Scott Fitzgerald and the play by Owen Drake; photographed by John F. Seitz; musical score by Robert Emmett Dolan; running time, 92 minutes.

Cast: Alan Ladd (*Jay Gatsby*), Betty Field (*Daisy Buchanan*), Barry Sullivan (*Tom Buchanan*), Macdonald Carey (*Nick Caraway*), Ruth Hussey (*Jordan Baker*), Howard da Silva (*Wilson*), Shelley Winters (*Myrtle Wilson*), Elisha Cook, Jr. (*Klipspringer*), Ed Begley (*Myron Lupus*), Henry Hull (*Dan Cody*), Carole Matthews (*Ella Cody*), Nicholas Joy (*Owl Man*), Tito Vuolo (*Mavromichaclis*).

F. Scott Fitzgerald died in Hollywood in 1940, at forty-four, tired and alcoholic. The Prophet of the Prohibition Era was not able to come to terms with life, and he particularly disliked working in the film capital. Sheila Graham touched upon Fitzgerald's discomfort as a movie writer in her *Beloved Infidel*, which was made into a not very successful picture in 1959, with Gregory Peck playing Fitzgerald.

Peck was not a good choice—a better one would have been Alan Ladd, an actor who shared Fitzgerald's tendency to introspection and alcoholic retreat. Ladd was fascinated by Fitzgerald's writings, and for some years he hounded Paramount to cast him in the part of Jay Gatsby. They finally let him have his way and Ladd turned in one of his better performances, although Fitzgerald enthusiasts felt that the picture failed to fully capture the bittersweet flavor of the original.

The Great Gatsby was dramatized by Owen Davis in 1926 and did only fair business as a Broadway play. Later that year it was made into a silent movie, with Warner Baxter as Gatsby and Lois Wilson as Daisy. As this book goes to press a new version has been released, starring Robert Redford and Mia Farrow. Its generally poor reviews and lukewarm public reception appear to ensure the 1949 version's place in film history.

Betty Field, Alan Ladd and Barry Sullivan.

Jay Gatsby is a man who rises from poverty to wealth and finds little happiness in it. While in the service in the First World War, he becomes engaged to a social beauty, Daisy (Betty Field), but when he returns from the war he finds her married to a rich playboy, Tom Buchanan (Barry Sullivan).

The embittered Gatsby plunges into business and makes a fortune providing liquor during prohibition. He buys a Long Island mansion near Daisy and contrives to see her. She eventually agrees to leave her husband, but one night, driving while drunk, she knocks down and kills the wife (Shelley Winters) of a gas station owner (Howard Da Silva). To shield her Gatsby takes the blame for the accident, and the husband, who despises the giddy social set, goes to the Gatsby home and shoots him to death.

The film, excellent in its feeling for the period and well photographed by John F. Seitz, derives most of its value from Alan Ladd's sadly appealing Gatsby. In playing a stoic loner, Ladd clearly knew the territory.

Elisha Cook, Jr., Alan Ladd and Ed Begley.

Ruth Hussey, Macdonald Carey, Betty Field and Alan Ladd.

Virginia Mayo and James Cagney.

White Heat

1949

A Warner Bros. Production; produced by Louis F. Edelman; directed by Raoul Walsh; screenplay by Ivan Goff and Ben Roberts, based on a story by Virginia Kellogg; photographed by Sid Hickox; musical score by Max Steiner; running time, 114 minutes.

Cast: James Cagney (*Cody Jarrett*), Virginia Mayo (*Verna Jarrett*), Edmond O'Brien (*Hank Fallon*), Margaret Wycherly (*Ma Jarrett*), Steve Cochran (*Big Ed Somers*), John Archer (*Philip Evans*), Wally Cassell (*Cotton Valetti*), Mickey Knox (*Het*

Kohler), Fred Clark (*the Trader*), G. Pat Collins (*the Reader*), Paul Guilfoyle (*Roy Parker*), Fred Coby (*Happy Taylor*), Ford Rainey (*Zuckie Hommell*), Robert Osterloh (*Tommy Ryley*), Ian MacDonald (*Bo Creel*).

In his first ten years in Hollywood James Cagney had specialized in playing cocky, pugnacious little tough guys in an affecting and oddly appealing manner. He played this kind of character so well that the public tended to believe that what they

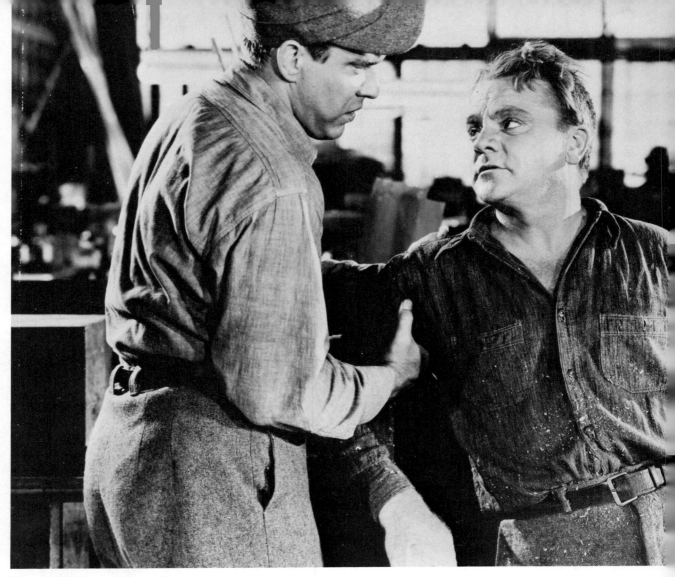

Edmond O'Brien and James Cagney.

were seeing was the real Cagney persona. Not so. Cagney was a keen-minded businessman, rather scholarly in private, and a superb actor. This became apparent in 1942, when he played George M. Cohan in *Yankee Doodle Dandy* and gave a brilliant performance, suitably recognized by an Oscar.

He left Warners and set up his own production company, but his projects fell far short of his expectations. In 1949 Cagney signed another contract with Warners, with whom he had always battled over money and properties, and it was decided to make a slambang gangster movie of the kind in which he had made his name. *White Heat* is, in fact, a summation of all the Cagney-Warners crime films and far superior to any of them. His role as a

vicious crook named Cody Jarrett is more dangerous and complex than any he had played in the thirties.

Jarrett is a psychotic personality, abnormally attached to his mother (Margaret Wycherly) and mistrustful of anyone else, including his wife (Virginia Mayo). His mistrust of his wife is justified—she has a yearning for his chief henchman (Steve Cochran).

To escape conviction for a major crime, Jarrett surrenders himself on a minor charge and goes to jail. There the state plants a detective, Hank Fallon (Edmond O'Brien), to win Jarrett's confidence and help him break out of jail.

Jarrett's tendency to insanity increases when he

James Cagney and Edmond O'Brien.

learns that his mother has been killed by his hench-man, who next plans to kill Jarrett and take his wife. The henchman meets a swift end.

In planning to rob the payroll of a chemical plant, Jarrett learns that Fallon is on the side of the law, but Fallon manages to get a message through to the police, and Jarrett goes to his death atop an exploding gas tank, screaming for the approval of his mother, "Top of the world!"

Even without James Cagney *White Heat* would be a rattling good crime movie, exciting and vivid in its pacing, thanks to the direction of action expert Raoul Walsh. But with Cagney and his extraordinary portrait of the evil, mercurial Jarrett, the film becomes a fascinating experience.

James Cagney and Margaret Wycherly.

Claude Jarman, Jr. and Elizabeth Patterson on location.

Intruder in the Dust

1949

An MGM Production; produced and directed by Clarence Brown; screenplay by Ben Maddow, based on the novel by William Faulkner; photographed by Robert Surtees; musical score by Adolph Deutsch; running time, 87 minutes.

Cast: David Brian (*John Gavin Stevens*), Claude Jarman, Jr. (*Chick Mallison*), Juano Hernandez (*Lucas Beauchamp*), Porter Hall (*Nub Gowrie*), Elizabeth Patterson (*Miss Habersham*), Charles Kemper (*Crawford Gowrie*), Will Geer (*Sheriff Hampton*), David Clark (*Vinson Gowrie*), Elzie Manuel (*Aleck*), Lela Bliss (*Mrs. Mallison*), Harry Hayden (*Mr. Mallison*), Harry Antrim (*Mr. Tubbs*), Dan White (*Will Legate*), Alberta Dismon (*Paralee*), R. X. Williams (*Mr. Lilley*), Ephraim and Edmund Lowe (*the Gowrie Twins*), Julia S. Marshbanks (*Molly Beauchamp*).

In 1949 Hollywood suddenly seemed to realize how tardy it was in respecting black Americans,

Claude Jarman, Jr. and Juano Hernandez

Dan White, Harry Antrim, Claude Jarman, Jr. and David Brian.

Chick Mallison (Claude Jarman, Jr.), who becomes his main ally in trying to bring justice.

The sheriff (Will Geer) also believes that Beauchamp is innocent, and a lawyer, John Gavin Stevens (David Brian), is persuaded to take the case and gradually becomes convinced of the desperate need to save his client.

However, the spirit and the tenacity of old Miss Habersham (Elizabeth Patterson) is what saves Beauchamp—she doggedly finds the evidence that pins the guilt on the real murderer.

Intruder in the Dust did not meet with great success, perhaps because it came late in the cycle of these new "tolerance" pictures. Perhaps, also, it was too much for many people to swallow. Certainly the scenes in which the townspeople prepare to lynch Beauchamp, as if it were a sports event, are among the most harrowing in a Hollywood movie. But quite apart from its admirable tackling of a disgraceful subject, the film is excellently constructed and gripping.

Will Geer (center).

who had seldom been fairly represented on the screen. Until this time blacks had been depicted as professional menials and low comics and, occasionally, credited for their contributions to popular music. Hollywood had hardly ever touched upon social inequality and discrimination. Now things began to change. Three 1949 films probed the thorny area of racial prejudice—*Pinky, Lost Boundaries,* and *Home of the Brave*—and one, *Intruder in the Dust,* actually had the courage to deal with mob violence and lynch law in the South.

The film was made in Oxford, Mississippi, using local people as extras, and it is much to the credit of producer-director Clarence Brown that he was able to get the townspeople to do his bidding, because it is not a pretty story.

This treatment of a William Faulkner novel pulls no punches in telling about a black man, Lucas Beauchamp (Juano Hernandez), who is accused of killing a white man and put in jail. Beauchamp is a respectable citizen who owns his own plot of land and carries himself with dignity, all of which adds to the resentment of many of the local whites. He has long befriended a white lad,

Ben Johnson, John Wayne and Fred Libbey.

She Wore a Yellow Ribbon

1949

An RKO-Radio-Argosy Production; produced by John Ford and Merian C. Cooper; directed by John Ford; screenplay by Frank S. Nugent and Lawrence Stallings, based on the story by James Warner Bellah; photographed in Technicolor by Winton Hoch; musical score by Richard Hageman; running time, 103 minutes.

Cast: John Wayne (*Captain Nathan Brittles*), Joanne Dru (*Olivia Dandridge*), John Agar (*Lieutenant Flint Cohill*), Ben Johnson (*Sergeant Tyree*), Harry Carey, Jr. (*Lieutenant Ross Pennell*), Victor McLaglen (*Sergeant Quincannon*), Mildred Natwick (*Abby Allshard*), George O'Brien (*Major Mack Allshard*), Arthur Shields (*Doctor O'Laughlin*), Harry Woods (*Karl Rynders*), Chief John Big-Tree (*Pony That Walks*), Noble Johnson (*Red Shirt*), Cliff Lyons (*Trooper Cliff*), Tom Tyler (*Mike Quayne*), Michael Dugan (*Sergeant Hochbauer*), Mickey Simpson (*Wagner*).

Fort Apache (1948), *She Wore a Yellow Ribbon* (1949), and *Rio Grande* (1950) form what is known as John Ford's U.S. Cavalry trilogy. Each stars John Wayne, and each paints a heroic-romantic picture of military life in the West in the two decades after the Civil War. The films are persuasive in their images and accounts, but Ford never claimed to be a historian, only a visual storyteller. His tales of the pony soldiers are cut from fictional cloth—with the possible exception of *Cheyenne Autumn* (1964), which came close to telling the truth about the brutal governmental mishandling of the Indians. Ironically, *Cheyenne Autumn* was the last of Ford's Westerns and the least successful.

Of the cavalry triology the most glowing is *She Wore a Yellow Ribbon*, magnificently color photographed in northern Arizona and full of shots reminiscent of Frederick Remington's paintings.

The screenplay by Frank Nugent and Lawrence Stalling is based on a story by James Warner Bellah, who was to the written Western word what Remington was to painting. It begins in 1876, just after the Custer defeat, when the Indian tribes were optimistic about being able to contain the white tide.

Harry Carey, Jr., Joanne Dru, John Wayne and John Agar.

John Wayne and George O'Brien.

263

Victor McLaglen, John Wayne, Ben Johnson and Mildred Natwick.

At Fort Stark, Captain Nathan Brittles (John Wayne), about to retire after long service, is commanded by Major Allshard (George O'Brien) to perform one final duty—to escort the Major's wife (Mildred Natwick) and her niece (Joanne Dru) to the end of the stagecoach line.

Reluctantly performing this simple chore, Brittles comes across evidence of increasing troubles with the Indians, and he and his charges return to the fort. This pleases a pair of lieutenants (John Agar and Harry Carey, Jr.), who are vying for the niece's hand.

The Indians leave their reservations, raid properties, and kill settlers, and Brittles takes it upon himself to settle the matter. He visits the main Indian camp and powwows with the old chief. The chief is unable to control his young bucks, and the soldiers are forced to quell them with military tactics.

His days as a soldier completed, Brittles bids farewell to his men, who present him with a gold watch, but he doesn't get far from the fort before a soldier overtakes him and hands him the commission he has sought as head of army scouts.

She Wore a Yellow Ribbon, mellowed with Fordian streaks of sentiment and respect for old-fashioned military life, may not be historically exact, but it is a readily acceptable idealization. This is how it all *should* have been.

265

Hedy Lamarr and Victor Mature.

Samson and Delilah

1949

A Paramount Production; produced and directed by Cecil B. De Mille; screenplay by Jesse L. Lasky, Jr., and Frederic M. Frank, based on Harold Lamb's adaptation of biblical material and the novel *Judge and Fool*, by Vladimir Jabotinsky; photographed in Technicolor by George Barnes; musical score by Victor Young; running time, 131 minutes.

Cast: Victor Mature (*Samson*), Hedy Lamarr (*Delilah*), George Sanders (*Saran of Gaza*), Angela Lansbury (*Semadar*), Henry Wilcoxon (*Ahtur*), Olive Deering (*Miriam*), Fay Holden (*Hazeleponit*), Julia Faye (*Hisham*), Russell Tamblyn (*Saul*), William Farnum (*Tubal*), Lane Chandler (*Teresh*), Moroni Olsen (*Targil*), Francis J. McDonald (*Storyteller*), William Davis (*Garmiskar*), John Miljan (*Lesh Lakish*).

Unlike John Ford, Cecil B. De Mille had pretentions of being a historian. Of his eighteen sound films twelve are built around historical situations.

In the 1940s he dealt with the early years of the *North West Mounted Police* (1940), the piracy that flourished along the Florida coasts in the early nineteenth century (*Reap the Wild Wind*, 1942), the adventures of a navy doctor in the South Pacific in World War II (*The Story of Dr. Wassell*), the exploits of colonists in prerevolutionary America (*Unconquered*), and then the affair of *Samson and Delilah*, as related in Judges 13–16 of the Old Testament.

De Mille was never afraid to be direct and obvious—he had the courage of his convictions —and in casting this picture he simply chose the most sensually beautiful actress and the most massively handsome actor then available in the Hollywood firmament—Lamarr and Mature. Who else?

In brief, the plot tells of a Danite of great strength and no finesse who aspires to marry a high-ranking Philistine, Semadar (Angela Lansbury). The Philistines take unkindly to this notion and revile Samson. The ensuing troubles result in Semadar's death, and her younger sister Delilah decides to take revenge on Samson. She feigns love for Samson in order to discover the secret of his

George Sanders, Hedy Lamarr, Angela Lansbury, Henry Wilcoxon and Victor Mature.

great strength, and when he is fully under her spell, he tells her. His strength lies in his hair, which she then cuts off when he falls into a drunken slumber.

However, by now Delilah has acquired some feeling for the innocent brute, and she demands that in arresting him the Philistines, particularly the crafty Saren of Gaza (George Sanders), himself covetous of Delilah, not kill Samson or touch his flesh. But it does occur to them to blind him and make him a slave.

As Samson's hair grows, his strength returns, and when he is brought into the temple to be ridiculed he pushes apart the main columns, causing the building to collapse and kill everyone.

De Mille was considered fair game by the critics, who found it easy to scoff at him, but that should not obsure his unusual skill as a filmmaker. He excelled in the highly difficult business of mounting vast spectacles and directing enormous crowds—feats few directors have been able to carry off with conviction. *Samson and Delilah* is visually magnificent, and in Mature and Lamarr, De Mille found perfect images for his epic tale.

268

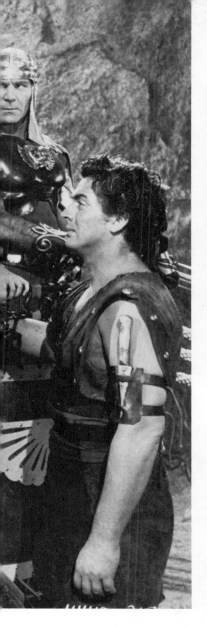

Hedy Lamarr,
Henry Wilcoxon and
George Sanders.

Anne Seymour, John Derek, Broderick Crawford and John Ireland.

All the King's Men

1949

A Columbia Production; produced, directed, and written by Robert Rossen, based on the novel by Robert Penn Warren; photographed by Burnett Guffey; musical score by Louis Gruenberg; running time, 109 minutes.

Cast: Broderick Crawford (*Willie Stark*), Joanne Dru (*Anne Stanton*), John Ireland (*Jack Burden*), John Derek (*Tom Stark*), Mercedes McCambridge (*Sadie Burke*), Shepperd Strudwick (*Adam Stanton*), Anne Seymour (*Lucy Stark*), Raymond Greenleaf (*Judge Stanton*), Ralph Dumke (*Tiny Duffy*), Katherine Warren (*Mrs. Burden*), Walter Burke (*Sugar Boy*), Will Wright (*Dolph Pillsbury*), Grandon Rhodes (*Floyd McEvoy*), H. C. Miller (*Pa Stark*), Richard Hale (*Hale*), and William Bruce (*Commissioner*).

Robert Rossen (1908–1966) might have had a more fruitful career in Hollywood had it not been for his involvement in politics. After ten years as a writer he turned director with *Johnny O'clock* in

1947 and later that year made an excellent picture about crookedness in boxing, *Body and Soul*. Unfortunately, that was also the year the film industry began to be ripped open by political witch hunts.

Rossen was indicted for alleged leftist sympathies. He was later cleared of the charges, but like many another artist, he found his reputation tarnished and his work opportunities diminished.

Ironically, the film for which Rossen is most remembered is a purely political entry, *All the King's Men*, which he wrote, directed, and produced. The film is a study in fascism and political corruption, basically the rise and fall of a backwoods rebel named Willie Stark. In the beginning Stark is hell bent on reform and justice for the underprivileged, but in time he becomes drunk with his own power.

The Pulitzer Prize-winning novel by Robert Penn Warren on which Rossen based his screenplay was clearly inspired by the antics of the former governor of Louisiana Huey Long, and the film made the parallel even sharper. Stark (Broderick Craw-

Broderick Crawford

Broderick Crawford, Raymond Greenleaf, John Ireland and Mercedes McCambridge.

ford) is gifted with the ability to persuade crowds with oratory. This ability quickly gets him elected to office. A jaundiced intellectual, Jack Burden (John Ireland), and a shrewd woman, Sadie Burke (Mercedes McCambridge), join his team to write his speeches and manage his campaign, and step by step Stark climbs the political ladder to the governor's mansion.

His ambition costs him his family life and the respect of his son (John Derek). Proved corruption in his administration leads to demands for his impeachment, but Stark manages to surmount the charges. He cannot, however, escape the bullets of an assassin (Shepperd Strudwick), whose father, a judge, Stark ruined.

All the King's Men surprised a great many people in Hollywood by winning an Oscar as the best film of 1949. Not surprising were the Oscars given Broderick Crawford and Mercedes McCambridge for their vital performances. Crawford had hitherto made a good living as a second lead in mostly nondescript pictures, but here he gave an electrifying portrait of a frightening political animal—hungry, brutal, and crafty. Robert Rossen's film continues to be a guidepost for other producers of political material and a warning to the rest of us.

272

Broderick Crawford and John Ireland.

Montgomery Clift and Olivia de Havilland.

The Heiress

1949

A Paramount Production; produced and directed by William Wyler; screenplay by Ruth and Augustus Goetz, based on the play by the Goetzes, suggested by the novel *Washington Square,* by Henry James; photographed by Leo Tover; musical score by Aaron Copland; running time, 115 minutes.

Cast: Olivia de Havilland (*Catherine Sloper*), Montgomery Clift (*Morris Townsend*), Ralph Richardson (*Doctor Austin Sloper*), Miriam Hopkins (*Lavinia Penniman*), Vanessa Brown (*Maria*), Mona Freeman (*Marian Almond*), Ray Collins (*Jefferson Almond*), Betty Linley (*Mrs. Montgomery*), Selena Royle (*Elizabeth Almond*), Paul Lees (*Arthur Townsend*), Harry Antrim (*Mr. Abeel*), Russ Conway (*Quintus*), Davis Thursby (*Geier*).

William Wyler, yet another of Hollywood's German-born giants, came to the full flowering of his talents in the 1940s. He began the decade with Gary Cooper's *The Westerner* (1940) and followed it with two of Bette Davis's best pictures, *The Letter* (1940) and *The Little Foxes* (1941). He next turned a basically trite piece of propaganda into a near classic, *Mrs. Miniver* (1942), and then joined the air corps as a documentary-film maker.

Returning to Hollywood Wyler made *The Best Years of Our Lives* (1946), the finest of all the "homecoming" pictures, and after taking a long rest of more than two years he tackled *The Heiress.*

The meticulous, tough-on-actors Wyler here devised a thoroughly authentic picture of upper-class New York life in the mid-nineteenth century and drew subtle performances from Sir Ralph Richardson, making his first appearance in an American film, and from Olivia de Havilland. Basil Rathbone and Wendy Hiller had played the roles on Broadway, but Paramount did not consider them strong enough to carry the leads in an expensive movie.

Part of the quality of this film comes from the wise decision to allow Ruth and Augustus Goetz, who had written the stage play based on Henry James's *Washington Square,* to be fully responsible

Olivia de Havilland and
Ralph Richardson.

Miriam Hopkins, Montgomery Clift, Ralph Richardson and Olivia de Havilland.

Montgomery Clift and Olivia de Havilland.

for the screenplay. Yet another factor was the choice of Aaron Copland to write the musical score, which earned him an Oscar.

The story is that of a naïve, plain, sheltered young woman, Catherine Sloper (Olivia de Havilland), whose wealthy doctor father (Richardson) has made known to her that he does not like her. At a ball she finds herself flatteringly attended by handsome Morris Townsend (Montgomery Clift). He asks if he may call on her, and she eagerly agrees.

The rapid courtship does not receive the approval of Doctor Sloper, who rightfully assumes that Morris is a fortune hunter. He objects to the marriage and tells Catherine that he will disinherit her if she proceeds. This makes little difference to her, but it makes a great deal of difference to Morris, who vanishes.

She asks her father to disinherit her, but he refuses, and Catherine gradually turns from being sweet natured to being hard. Her father's death causes her no sorrow, and years later, when Morris slyly returns to worm his way back into her affections, she seemingly surrenders. But when he returns to take her away he finds the front door bolted—forever.

Oliva de Havilland won her second Oscar for this performance, a deeply touching portrait of a gentle, thwarted woman. She had also been nominated for playing a mentally disturbed lady in the harrowing *The Snake Pit* (1948), and in both films she played down her own attractiveness.

276

Twelve O'Clock High

1949

A 20th Century-Fox Production; produced by Darryl F. Zanuck; directed by Henry King; screenplay by Cy Bartlett and Beirne Lay, Jr., based on the novel by Bartlett; photographed by Leon Shamroy; musical score by Alfred Newman; running time, 132 minutes.

Cast: Gregory Peck (*General Savage*), Hugh Marlowe (*Lieutenant Colonel Ben Gately*), Gary Merrill (*Colonel Davenport*), Millard Mitchell (*General Pritchard*), Dean Jagger (*Major Stovell*), Robert Arthur (*Sergeant McIllhenny*), Paul Stewart (*Captain Kaiser*), John Kellogg (*Major Cobb*), Robert Patten (*Lieutenant Bishop*), Lee McGregor (*Lieutenant Zimmerman*), Sam Edwards (*Birdwell*), Roger Anderson (*Interrogation Officer*), John Zilly (*Sergeant Ernie*).

Gregory Peck

Movies about the Second World War continued to be made in Hollywood long after the war but they were free of the gung-ho character of those made during the conflict. Now the moviemakers could take a more adult and intelligent look at war and its effects. In 1949 Hollywood produced two exceptionally good films about the American bombing of Germany—*Command Decision* and *Twelve O'clock High*. Neither glorified bombing, but both focused on the anxieties of command and the stress and strain of those involved in bombing. Of the two, *Twelve O'clock High* (air-force jargon for "bombers over target") is the more interesting because it has less talk and more action and skillfully incorporates actual aviation footage shot by Allied and German cameramen.

The central character, Brigadier General Savage (Gregory Peck), was based on Major General Frank A. Armstrong, who led the first American daylight bombing assaults against Germany.

Sy Bartlett and Beirne Lay, Jr., had little interference from the studio in adapting their novel into a screenplay. The story is told in the form of a flashback as an ex air corps major (Dean Jagger) visits London some years after the war and takes a side trip to the airfield where the 918th Bomb Group, U.S. 8th Air Corps, was stationed and where he was the adjutant to General Savage.

The airfield is deserted and untended, and as he looks at it his mind wanders. He thinks back to the days when the young general was put in command, replacing duty-weary Colonel Davenport (Gary Merrill) and getting himself disliked for being a martinent.

Within a week of Savage's arrival most of his pilots have asked for transfers, but with time they come to respect him for his efficiency in running a greatly difficult operation.

After a while the same thing happens to Savage as to his predecessor—he grows protective about his men and becomes identified with them, making it increasingly hard for him to send them to dangers that often result in their deaths. Inevitably he breaks down and has to be restrained from wanting to fly with his men.

Gregory Peck understandably looks upon his role in *Twelve O'clock High* as one of his best. Fox chieftain Darryl F. Zanuck cared enough about this one to take personal command of the production, and he assigned three of his top employees, all Fox veterans, to give it their best—director Henry King, photographer Leon Shamroy, and composer Alfred Newman. Their best made this a great film.

278

Gary Merrill, Gregory Peck and Millard Mitchell.

Gregory Peck and Millard Mitchell.

Gary Merrill, Hugh Marlowe, Dean Jagger and Gregory Peck.

FREE!

Citadel Film Series Catalog

From James Stewart to Moe Howard and The Three Stooges, Woody Allen to John Wayne, The Citadel Film Series is America's largest film book library.

Now with more than 125 titles in print, books in the series make perfect gifts—for a loved one, a friend, or yourself!

We'd like to send you, free of charge, our latest full-color catalog describing the Citadel Film Series in depth. To receive the catalog, call 1-800-447-BOOK or send your name and address to:

Citadel Film Series/Carol Publishing Group
Distribution Center B
120 Enterprise Avenue
Secaucus, New Jersey 07094

The titles you'll find in the catalog include:
The Films Of...

Alan Ladd
Alfred Hitchcock
All Talking! All Singing!
    All Dancing!
Anthony Quinn
The Bad Guys
Barbara Stanwyck
Barbra Streisand:
    The First Decade
Barbra Streisand:
    The Second Decade
Bela Lugosi
Bette Davis
Bing Crosby
Black Hollywood
Boris Karloff
Bowery Boys
Brigitte Bardot
Burt Reynolds
Carole Lombard
Cary Grant
Cecil B. DeMille
Character People
Charles Bronson
Charlie Chaplin
Charlton Heston
Chevalier
Clark Gable
Classics of the Gangster
    Film
Classics of the Horror Film
Classics of the Silent Screen
Cliffhanger
Clint Eastwood
Curly: Biography of a
    Superstooge
Detective in Film
Dick Tracy
Dustin Hoffman
Early Classics of the
    Foreign Film

Elizabeth Taylor
Elvis Presley
Errol Flynn
Federico Fellini
The Fifties
The Forties
Forgotten Films
    to Remember
Frank Sinatra
Fredric March
Gary Cooper
Gene Kelly
Gina Lollobrigida
Ginger Rogers
Gloria Swanson
Great Adventure Films
Great British Films
Great French Films
Great German Films
Great Romantic Films
Great Science Fiction Films
Great Spy Films
Gregory Peck
Greta Garbo
Harry Warren and the
    Hollywood Musical
Hedy Lamarr
Hello! My Real Name Is
Henry Fonda
Hollywood Cheesecake:
    60 Years of Leg Art
Hollywood's Hollywood
Howard Hughes in Hollywood
Humphrey Bogart
Ingrid Bergman
Jack Lemmon
Jack Nicholson
James Cagney
James Stewart
Jane Fonda
Jayne Mansfield

Jeanette MacDonald and
    Nelson Eddy
Jewish Image in American
    Films
Joan Crawford
John Garfield
John Huston
John Wayne
John Wayne Reference
    Book
John Wayne Scrapbook
Judy Garland
Katharine Hepburn
Kirk Douglas
Lana Turner
Laurel and Hardy
Lauren Bacall
Laurence Olivier
Lost Films of the
    Fifties
Love in the Film
Mae West
Marilyn Monroe
Marlon Brando
Moe Howard and The
    Three Stooges
Montgomery Clift
More Character People
More Classics of the
    Horror Film
More Films of the '30s
Myrna Loy
Non-Western Films of
    John Ford
Norma Shearer
Olivia de Havilland
Paul Newman
Paul Robeson
Peter Lorre
Pictorial History of Science
    Fiction Films

Pictorial History of Sex
    in Films
Pictorial History of War
    Films
Pictorial History of the
    Western Film
Rebels: The Rebel Hero
    in Films
Rita Hayworth
Robert Redford
Robert Taylor
Ronald Reagan
The Seventies
Sex in the Movies
Sci-Fi 2
Sherlock Holmes
Shirley MacLaine
Shirley Temple
The Sixties
Sophia Loren
Spencer Tracy
Steve McQueen
Susan Hayward
Tarzan of the Movies
They Had Faces Then
The Thirties
Those Glorious Glamour Years
Three Stooges Book of Scripts
Three Stooges Book of Scripts,
    Vol. 2
The Twenties
20th Century Fox
Warren Beatty
W. C. Fields
Western Films of John Ford
West That Never Was
William Holden
William Powell
Woody Allen
World War II

1-29-92 Midwest 12.95 #48597